GW00771429

IT'S A SHE

A Tale of Life, Loss and Love

Magdalene Matthews

Xulon Press
2301 Lucien Way #415
Maitland, FL 32751
407.339.4217
www.xulonpress.com

Paperback ISBN-13: 978-1-66282-294-0
Ebook ISBN-13: 978-1-66282-295-7

Table of Contents

Section Four
LIFE LESSONS

Praise for "It's a She"

"*Magdalene captures the Liberian experience of conflict from the unique vantage point as the child of a politician, whose upbringing was deeply sandwiched by the activities of a revolution that sought to bring about change in the national political landscape.*

Through the lens of her childhood, she expresses the complexities of Liberia's politics, amplifies the unheard and untold stories of her generation, and echoes the impact of the nation's prolonged civil unrest and the continued journey to healing and reconciliation.

Hers is a story of hope, renewal, and a challenge to the narratives of the Liberia we want and the Africa we aspire to see."

Facia Boyenoh Harris, Gender Activist

"*It's a She" is not your average memoir. It is a work of classical finesse, interweaving life, love, loss, politics, and scholarly repertoire in a chilling, exhilarating narrative. It walks you through the struggle of a country, the dream of a girl child, a garden of broken roses, valleys of shattered dreams, and the uphill climb up a mountain of hope. Through the eyes of Magdalene Matthews, we see Liberia as it unveils the hidden cracks in its socio-political dichotomies, class struggle, and power switches.*

Magdalene gives us a rare glimpse of her father, a man in the middle of the struggle for political pluralism in Liberia. Gabriel Baccus Matthews is regarded as the father of multiparty democracy in Liberia, sometimes seen as a polarizing figure in Liberia's political sphere by his critics, a political change-maker by his admirers, a sacrificial lamb slaughtered on the altar of democracy by others. However history remembers Baccus Matthews, Magdalene gives insider perspectives to the character, mind, and life of the man once standing in the way of the ancient political establishment in Liberia.

Magdalene captures Liberia, from the mundane—cuisine, everyday Pidgin English, politics and history, to the global space of arts and poetry, literature, fashion, and life.

"It's a She" provides hope for single women nursing hopes for tomorrow, juggling society's expectations and criticisms, to individuals pursuing hope and healing, to our dear country Liberia, still seeking answers in the depths of its soul."

Lekpele M. Nyamalon, Author, *Scary Dreams*

"It's a She" provides balanced historical perspectives of Liberia from someone who lived through those times. It gives insight into the real world of children born to political figures—the challenges they face and the pressures of being held accountable for their parents' choices. It is a captivating read that keeps you glued to a coherent, descriptive story of a resilient young woman determined to break the glass ceiling and write her own story.

S. Gentry Taylor, Visionary & Founder, Agents of Change

"It's a She" is a brilliant synergy between Magdalene Matthews' life and the nation of Liberia. It immerses us into a young lady's challenges and experiences, morphing into a bold and confident woman, wife, mother, and professional. The book is a merchant of hope with a compelling message— you can endure so much and still anticipate a better future.

The narrative also shares personal perspectives on what it meant to grow up in the shadow of politics. "It's a She" is a testimonial forged in the fires of life with an inspiring message of persistence until the very end.

Bryan Muthetia, IT and Cyber Security Specialist

"It's a She" tells the compelling story of overcoming barriers, resilience, and succeeding against the odds. As the author's older brother, I have watched her navigate life with brilliant grace, always pushing to higher heights. Her life and accomplishments share lessons that can be an inspiration to us all.

Martin Matthews, Financial Advisor & Author

"This book is a compass to every dreamer that is dealing with the challenges of change. Each chapter is pregnant with a fresh dose of inspiration, courage and resilience to survive life's obstacles and still come out on top. The treasure within you will be provoked. Your eyes will be opened to see possibilities in impossible situations. This, is definitely a must read."

Vicky Mwangi, Life Coach & Visionary, Mrembo Women's Ministry

To Jordan and Mishan,
May you find the courage and strength to rise above
anything life brings.

Acknowledgments

This book is the product of 30 years of life and 10 years of intentional growth and introspection. I owe an immense debt of gratitude to my family, friends, and support system for their unflinching love, prayers, and encouragement, leading to where I am today. This tale of life, loss, love and lessons learned could not have been without your help.

As you read through and recognize your footprints, that is my way of saying thank you for everything you added to help shape my life's narrative.

To my parents, Gabriel Baccus Matthews (of blessed memory) and Helena Ajavon Kidio, thank you for investing love, time, and resources in ensuring I learned the value of education, broadened my worldview, and emerged with a remarkable story to tell along the way.

To my husband Dennis Ofori-Kuma, who covered so many fronts, allowing me to dedicate much-needed time and attention to this project, thank you for always being the wind beneath my wings. To my son and daughter, Jordan and Mishan, my prayer for you is that someday you find your own voice and use it for good.

To my brothers, who have encouraged and sharpened my ideas over the years, you all share in this story. Thank you for entrusting me to tell it to the world from our unique vantage point.

To my dynamic team of cross-cultural reviewers, who contributed time, inputs, and enthusiasm to refine this manuscript, I owe an immense debt of gratitude. Thank you:

Joseph & Helena Kidio, USA

Martin & Chelsea Matthews, USA

Jerry Matthews, USA

Kate Clarke, USA

Jocelia Kidio, USA

Romeo Clarke, Jr., Liberia

S. Gentry Taylor, Liberia

Georgina Harris-Neufville, Liberia

Lekpele M. Nyamalon, Liberia

Facia B. Harris, Liberia

Kermi & Musu Gopeya, Sr., Liberia

Romeo & Nomor Clarke, Sr., Liberia

Kofi Annoh Mensah, Ghana

Sylvia Akonai-Otoo, Ghana (of blessed memory)

Emily Milisa Juma, Kenya

Bryan Mutethia, Kenya

Vanessa Eva Vinya, Kenya

Bishop Eric and Reverend Vicky Mwangi, Kenya

To my indefatigable editor, Susan Mbogoh, thank you for the passion you brought to this project. Your eagerness to get this manuscript to print made the editing process an enjoyable one.

To God Almighty, I owe my most profound gratitude. Without Him, there would be no tale to tell.

"Maybe you've been assigned this mountain to show others it can be moved."

Unknown

Prologue

Huh? It's a "SHE"?

"A day will come when the story inside you will want to breathe on its own. That's when you'll start writing[1]."
Sarah Noffke, Novelist

Accra, 2016

It was a warm evening in the Ghanaian capital, Accra, and there I was, on the magnificent grounds of the Independence Square, contemplating. On the road nearby, cars drive along swiftly on the buzzing street—commuters heading home after a long week's work. Over the years, Ghana had evolved from being the country I traveled to for school; into becoming my second home and a haven where many intellectual and creative sparks would be ignited in my soul. Ghana allured me with its reticent charm, imposing shoulders, and piercing brown eyes, a gaze that has held me captive ever since.

The Independence Square in Osu had become a reflective sanctuary I would often retreat to whenever life hit a snag. Here I was, once again, standing on the sacred birthplace of

Africa's post-colonial liberation, nursing my wounds after yet another of life's brutal battles.

The power, presence, and echoes of my surroundings envelope me even as a soothing breeze rushes through my cascading brown hair. The sun, slowly yet ever so majestically, makes her gentle exit from the evening sky. A few meters away lies the vast expanse of the Atlantic Ocean, its waves beating rhythmically against the historic shore. To the right, towering in the ombré sky is the monumental Independence Arch. Inscribed on it, the words "Freedom and Justice" scream into the universe, inches below a striking, 5-sided black star, the symbol of the Republic. The wind blows, the waves break, the sun sets, alone in my thoughts, I feel it. History awakes in response to my presence. Suddenly, I am no longer alone...

As far as the eye can see, the crowd engulfed me, pushing hard on every side. White handkerchiefs wave in jubilation. Sweaty hands and arms rub up against me; there is hardly enough room to stand. Every other sound is silenced by deafening shouts of celebration. Thunderous vibrations of thousands of feet dancing and stomping against the pavement created a magnetic field so strong you could taste it.

Call it a vision or epiphany; in an instant, it was March 6th, 1957, and I was there, standing in the cradle of time, somehow teleported to relive the glory of that single sunset that would change every other. I look up, and there he was, standing regally on the podium, flanked by comrades, in a pristine, white hat and tailored smock, proclaiming the words that would rewrite history:

> *"At long last, the battle has ended. And thus, Ghana, your beloved country, is free forever[2]!"*

Kwame Nkrumah's ebony skin glistened under the setting sun[a]. He personified a hunger, embodied a passion for an Africa I had never seen. Wisdom poured out of his lips; purpose oozed out of his pores. Every heart within earshot held on to his every word, standing, staring, expecting. For the first time in history, the national anthem echoed across the vast expanse of the coastal shore as the newly minted Ghanaian flag climbed its way up a pole, into the evening sky, in full view of all. Raw emotions well up inside me. Silent tears slowly found their way down my cheeks. The tingly sensations of hopes fulfilled rushed down my spine. Then and there, I became one with the moment, one with the people, hearts beating as one. Overcome with emotion, I find myself subdued by an idealistic vision for a continent I was born in, had lived in all my life, but only now began to see through Nkrumah's eyes.

Once hoisted, the Black Star waved in the wind, announcing the birth of Africa's first post-colonial independent state— marking the end of an era. Fireworks followed, lighting up the night, setting the stage for festivities. Then, just as quickly as it had appeared, the historical scene vanished, thrusting me back into the present. This time, I take in my surroundings with a greater sense of awe, humbled by fresh revelation.

On those sun-kissed grounds, post-colonial Africa was born. On those grounds, Ghana became an independent nation. On those grounds, for the last six decades, Presidents have been empowered to rule; new eras charted; new chapters started. That day, standing on those hallowed grounds, emerged a tremendous urge to raise my voice; to speak, to share, to write, to set free, to be. Somewhere locked in the

---

a Kwame Nkrumah was the first Prime Minister and President of Ghana (1957-1966). He was also a strong proponent of Pan-Africanism, "the idea that peoples of African descent have common interests and should be unified." Source: Encyclopedia Britannica

clefts of my soul was a compelling story, longing to breathe on its own. The story inside me begged to be told. I could no longer ignore it. With gushing inspiration, I open a notebook and frantically begin to write.

***

"Teta, Teta, my child, we have to go to the hospital now."

"The baby is not well-positioned; I have tried my best, but I can't deliver this baby here at the clinic. It's too risky! We have to get you to the hospital!"

"But the pain is too much, Ma Bea... The baby is already coming; I can feel it!"

"Wait... let me push again... Let me push..."

My mother let out a scream as another contraction rushed through the core of her being. Drenched in sweat, it had been several hours since she fell into labor. The earlier walking exercises and past childbirth experience, doing nothing to lessen the excruciating pain.

"No, Teta!!! Wait! Do not push now! Stop! Let's get you to Catholic Hospital," the seasoned midwife interjected.

Frantic, she ran outside into the clinic's waiting area: "Who went to call Mr. Matthews?" she asked Mom's cousin, who, along with two other relatives, had been outside awaiting the good news.

"We need to get Teta to Catholic Hospital right away! We are running into complications! I cannot deliver this baby here; I need nurses to help. Go get a taxi now!"

Within minutes, one relative dashed out of the house to get a hold of Dad. Another hailed a taxi to scuttle Mom to the hospital. St. Joseph's Catholic Hospital was a mere

15 minutes' drive from Ma Bea's Midwife Center in Congo Town, in the suburbs of the Liberian capital, Monrovia. Given the panic of the moment, the minutes could have pretty much been hours. It was March 1987, long before the cell phone era; emergency calls such as these required physically getting ahold of someone. Mom was in hard labor, and I was well on the way, breached, and incredibly determined to enter the world buttocks first.

Ma Bea, my mother's highly experienced midwife, with her burgeoning clinic, had assisted mothers in bringing forth hundreds of babies into the world in her lifetime, including my older brother Martin, just three years before. She instinctively knew which deliveries she could safely manage and which cases she wouldn't take a risk with outside an equipped hospital. My birth turned out to be more complicated than either she or my mother had anticipated. Their well-laid plans for an in-clinic delivery had to be quickly squashed as I made my ungracious entry at the St. Joseph's Catholic Hospital on the morning of Saturday, March 21st, 1987, into my mother's fatigued embrace.

Dad arrived at the hospital just in time for the good news. With four sons under his belt, by the time I came along, there was no question about the gender of the baby—it could only be another boy. He was known to jokingly say he couldn't "make any girls." So, while Mom spent her entire pregnancy anxiously praying for a baby girl, Dad spent those 9 months encouraging her to manage her expectations. At that moment, his concerns centered only on Mom's welfare after such a stressful ordeal. Once in her room, Dad placed a tender hand on her forehead:

"How are you, old lady?" He affectionately asked. "Thank you for our baby." He smiled, bending over and planting a soft kiss on her sweat-drenched forehead.

Her droopy eyes and tired smile indicated the magnitude of exertion from just hours before.

"My goodness! I am so tired, Gabriel. Martin was rough because he was so small, but this one had so many complications! She gave me such a hard time!" She feebly replied.

Handkerchief in hand, he reassuringly wiped her face,

"It's ok, you did so well. So happy you are both alright. Just rest now; it is all going to be ok."

Suddenly, soaking up her response like a thrust of lightning, he jumped to his feet, wide-eyed:

"Huh? It's a "SHE?""

Ecstatic, he rushed out to catch his first glimpse of his little girl. On that sunny March afternoon, as I cried my first cry, I broke the mold. I was born the exception to the rule. I changed the narrative. In the pack of boys, I emerged, a SHE.

***

Over the years, the words "It's a "SHE" have remained iconic in the narrative of my life. Not only do they capture my father's enthusiastic reaction upon discovering the gender of his newborn baby, but they also describe my warm, fuzzy feelings when I, too, found out I was having a baby girl. For all the joys it has evoked over the years, ironically, "It's a She" has also been a glass ceiling. It has been an invisible lid, a predefined limitation instituted to keep me and thousands of other women and girls in our place—whatever societal norms, cultural beliefs, unconscious biases, and unspoken prejudices have determined that place to be.

"It's a She" has come to be a pervasive thread running through the different chapters of my life, taking on diverse meanings at different seasons and when spoken by various people. It also summarizes the most poignant illustration of my life's journey thus far.

A lioness in the Serengeti of life, "It's a She," is my history of the hunt; my story of life, loss, love, and coming of age as a young African woman, as the daughter of a leading political player, in a conflicted Liberia, seeking to emerge from war into an era of peace and self-determination.

This book describes my journey of growth, maturity, and progressive self-awareness in the pursuit of my dreams from a starry-eyed teenage girl into a daring young woman. It represents my recollection of tests, trials, and triumphs along life's trajectory, that have collectively led me to where I am now.

"It's a She" is a captivating kaleidoscope of life through the prism of my experiences. It's an inspiring call to embrace obstacles without necessarily looking for solutions but unraveling lessons. As a narrative, it transcends the genre of self-help and memoir to evoke an intriguing symphony of life across seasons.

While my life's journey is still unfolding, I am convinced that my story so far carries a compelling message of hope, resilience, and renewal that will inspire and encourage you along your own journey towards the sun.

Magdalene Matthews

Introduction

Historical Context

"If asked to describe my homeland in a sentence, I might say something like this: Liberia is a wonderful, beautiful, mixed-up country struggling mightily to find itself[3]."

Ellen Johnson-Sirleaf, 24th President, Republic of Liberia

It's impossible to recollect my life's journey without situating it within the context of Liberia's complex history.

Liberia was founded in the 1800s as a colonial experiment on liberty. Freed slaves in the United States were repatriated to the western coast of Africa to survive and thrive. An alternative to emancipation, settling in Liberia was a replica of the American colonial experiment on religious freedom led by the Pilgrims and Puritans in New England a century before. In a stark parallel to Christopher Columbus' discovery of the New World, the "discovered" land had long been discovered. It was occupied by indigenous tribes of African natives, with their own cultures, religions, and way of life; the occupation of which would not be without its share of conflict, an anthropological survival of the fittest, with one group ultimately seeking rulership over the other.

One historical account narrates:

"Before the arrival of the colonists from the United States, Liberian territory was home to about 750,000 inhabitants comprising 16 indigenous ethnic groups of the Niger-Congo family. These groups further subdivided into 4 ethnic clusters based on cultural and linguistic similarities: the Kwa (Bassa, Belle, Dey, Grebo, Krahn, and Kru); Mende-Fu (Gbandi, Gio/Dan, Kpelle, Loma, Mano/Ma, and Mende); Mende-Tan (Mandingo and Vai) and Mel (Gola and Kissi)[4]."

In the early part of the 18th century, these ethnic groups lived surrounded in an area yet unclaimed by imperial Great Britain and France. It is on this colonially unclaimed land, between the French colonies of la Côte d'Ivoire and Guinea and the British colony of Sierra Leone, that in 1822, the American Colonization Society (ACS) facilitated the arrival of the first shipload of free slaves to Africa from the United States[5]. When slavery was abolished in the US, numerous moral and economic questions arose surrounding emancipation versus advancing the Liberian colonial experiment[6]. This would greatly influence the establishment of Africa's first independent state, and subsequently, ACS[b] operations in Liberia[7].

In an 1854 address, Abraham Lincoln stated his own moral conflict between the economic realities of transporting

---

b The American Colonization Society was founded in 1817 by Robert Finley, a Presbyterian minister, to support the voluntary emigration of free slaves back to the African continent. It is believed that the ACS was established to appease two opposing groups; one group of philanthropists and abolitionists that wanted slaves to be free and returned to their motherland and another group of slave owners who feared their numbers and wanted them expelled from the United States. Both groups feared that free black slaves would not be able to assimilate in white American society. Some blacks, for their part, saw colonization as their only chance at freedom, fearing that black Americans would never attain full equality in the US. Others believed African-Americans should stay in the US to fight against slavery and obtain legal rights as American citizens, a narrative which remains relevant in the 21st century. The organization later functioned as a Liberian aid society until it dissolved in 1964.

free slaves back to the African continent and the racial implications of their socio-political emancipation in the US:

> *"My first impulse would be to free all the slaves and send them to Liberia --to their own native land. But a moment's reflection would convince me that whatever of high hope (as I think there is) there may be in this, in the long run, its sudden execution is impossible. If they were all landed there in a day, they would all perish in the next ten days; and there are not surplus shipping and surplus money enough in the world to carry them there in many times ten days.*
>
> *What then? Free them all, and keep them among us as underlings? Is it quite certain that this betters their condition? I think I would not hold one in slavery, at any rate, yet the point is not clear enough for me to denounce people upon. What next? Free them, and make them politically and socially, our equals? My own feelings will not admit of this; and if mine would, we well know that those of the great mass of white people will not[8]."*

The scale tipped in favor of repatriation. Thus, between 1820 to 1867, the American Colonization Society would send more than 13,000 freed slaves to Liberia[9]. As several historical accounts indicate, much like the Pilgrims' arrival at Plymouth in the United States in 1620, the land, now formally recognized as Liberia, though uncolonized by imperial powers, was home to hundreds of thousands of inhabitants[10]. The resulting geopolitical divide between those whom "the love of liberty brought[c]" on boats to the land and those whom "the love of liberty met" there would create an "Indigenous/Native Liberian" and "Americo-

---

c 'The Love of Liberty Brought Us Here" is the national motto of the Republic of Liberia.

Liberian" dichotomy, the infamous "Country" vs. "Congo" dynamic that would characterize much of Liberia's near 200-year history.

Legitimized by the US, the arriving settlers established a governing structure that would rule the nation for over a hundred years. Former Liberian President Ellen Johnson Sirleaf (2006-2018), in her memoir, *This Child Will Be Great*, writes:

> "The settlers of modern-day Liberia decided they would plant their feet in Africa but keep their faces turned squarely toward the United States. This stance would trigger a profound alienation between themselves and the indigenous peoples upon whose shores they had arrived and among whom they would build their new home. Alienation would lead to disunity; disunity would lead to a deeply cleaved society. That cleavage would set the stage for all the terror and bloodshed to come[11]."

US Military historian Brian Shellum, who chronicles the activities of African-American Officers in Liberia from 1910-1942, also writes:

> "Essentially, the United States extended its newfound imperial reach and dollar diplomacy to cover Liberia, defending an Americo-Liberian colonial government against encroachment and partition by Britain and France. At the same time, the Americo-Liberian minority who ruled in Monrovia employed the African American officers to subjugate the indigenous people living in the hinterland, the word generally used by Americo-Liberians for the tribal areas inland from the coastal settlements[12]."

By 1904, the 15th President of Liberia, Arthur Barclay (1904-1912), in his 1st inaugural address, would weigh in on Liberia's historical complexities:

"We cannot develop the interior effectively until a satisfactory understanding with the resident populations is arrived at. The efforts, which we have, in the past, made to coerce these populations by arms, have deservedly failed. Government must rest on the consent of the governed. We made a great initial mistake at the beginning of our national career. We sought to obtain and did succeed in grasping an enormous mass of territory, but we neglected to conciliate the populations and attach the resident populations to our interests[13]."

He added: "Our old attitude of indifference towards the native populations must be dropped." President Arthur Barclay saw the failure to conciliate the indigenous populations to the governing Americo-Liberian interests as a grave systemic weakness that needed urgent redress.

As unsettling as this part of our national history is, several accounts point to Liberia's binary social structure from inception as one of the root causes of the undercurrent of tensions and distrust, eventually escalating to a civil crisis a century and a half later.

From 1989 to 2003, the Liberian Civil War would only deepen this divide to ethnic groupings, with various indigenous groups forming factions against the others. This would give rise to ethnic chasms within the nation's fabric, requiring concerted action towards national reconciliation for decades to come.

The Truth and Reconciliation Commission (TRC)[d], in its concluding report, put it this way:

> *"Liberia's triumphant and tortuous history of conflict did not begin in January 1979 or end on October 14th, 2003. Rather, the historical antecedents are woven deeply into its troubled socio-political and psychological culture[14]."*

Over half a century later, the socio-economic rift established from the nation's origins would only widen. Liberia's century-old ethnic tensions would, regrettably, escalate, resulting in the 1979 rice riots, 1980 coup, and protracted civil crisis from 1989-2003.

On the brink of these tumultuous conflict years, my generation comes along, childhood witnesses to a nation in flames.

---

d The Truth and Reconciliation Commission (TRC) of Liberia (2005-2010), was a Legislative-enacted organization created in May 2005 to "promote national peace, security, unity and reconciliation" by investigating more than 20 years of civil conflict in the country and to report on gross human rights violations that occurred in Liberia between January 1979 and 14 October 2003. The TRC sought to provide a forum to address issues of impunity and allow victims and perpetrators of human rights violations to share their experiences, thereby creating a clear picture of the past to facilitate genuine healing and reconciliation. The Liberian TRC came to a conclusion in 2010, filing a final report and recommending relevant actions by national authorities to ensure responsibility and reparations. Source: The TRC Mandate

SECTION 1

LIFE

On the Back of History[15]

(For Liberia)

On the back of history
Came a small colony
A home of the Negroes
A land for them to smile
The first little country
In the breast of Africa

On the back of history
came men and women
spurred by will and valor,
one people united in adversity
when bullied by the bulldozers
They stood strong, arms under arms,
and declared a free nation

On the back of history, came Maryland,
creeping, crawling, crying to join her
brothers and sisters in love as a nation

On the back of history
came men and women of color
Roaming Africa for a land to rest
and to live and to call home.
They came from distant kingdoms
Some from Ancient Ghana, Mali,
or the Songhay empire
These daughters and sons of traders,
came in search of a place to call home

On the back of history
came the sons of King Sao Boso,
King Long Peter; the sons of Bob Gray;
the sons of Matilda Newport
sailing on the back of history on the
Mayflower, Elisabeth, Alligator, Cora
Our ancestors dreamed that one day,
their children would sit down together
void of tribe or ethnicity and write the stories
of their fathers with a lens clearer than any
binoculars for our country is a tye-dye nation
All sixteen tribes came with one voice
From cape Mesurado, to Bushrod Island
From Lofa to Nimba;
Bong to Grand Cape
Mount;

From Grand Gedeh to Grand Bassa;
someday, we'll see the faces of our neighbors
trooping to our land.
This time, not for slaves,
but to see the shores of Bushrod Island
where the men of color lived;
to see the shores
of Lake Piso;
to wander behind the forest of the
Sapo Park;
to picnic on the sides of Kpatawee,
all along the mangrove swamps;
and tropical rainforests

Then, we will ring the bell of our chorus
The love of Liberty
Brought us here!

Lekpele M. Nyamalon, Poet and Author

IT'S A SHE

***

Chapter 1

The 90s

"Liberia was like a pot of water that had been put on the stove, at a slow boil and forgotten about[16]."

Helene Cooper, New York Times Journalist, and Author

From the minute I took my first breath, I inhaled the rich oxygen of politics. It was there, poignant in the warm bosom that snuggled me to sleep at night and embedded in the fingers that held my tiny hands as I took my first steps. It was the constant topic of conversation at the table during breakfast and the crowning discourse over dinner. Like the ever-present mint green paint hugging the walls of our home, politics perfused my life from childhood.

Born in the late 1980s and growing up in Liberia in the 1990s, most of my childhood was spent either escaping from or surviving civil conflict, with very few interludes of peace. It was like living through an endless game of musical chairs, with different warring factions, to the tune of bullets and mayhem, fighting for the single coveted seat of state power. By the time the deadly music ceased, 14 years had flown by; with them, our childhood. We were now adults, disillusioned, and dealing with varying degrees of trauma, trying to gather the pieces of our shattered innocence.

Whenever I close my eyes to reflect on my childhood, like oil above water, certain scenes rush to the surface of my recollection. I see pictures of escape, images of fear, a slideshow of thousands of people walking through the streets with their belongings on their heads, and terrified children clutching tightly to their hands. From the year I turned two until my 16th birthday, Liberia was at war.

Given the resurgence of violent conflict in the 1990s, peace deals were often brokered around appeasing the warring factions. Transitional governments were formed with rebel leaders heading strategic ministries or having Vice Chairmanship roles headed by a supposedly neutral Chairperson. Not surprising then that the 90s were dubbed the era of "warlord politics." My earliest recollection of these dynamics at play and how they would spill over into our lives began in early 1995 and concretized by April 1996. My older brother, Martin, shares this compelling account of an attack at our house on January 14, 1995.

Liberia, 1995

"Don't shoot at them; shoot in the air!" Dad shouted.

This day a group of rebels attacked our home and exploded a grenade in our front-yard in Liberia. It was January 14th, 1995. I was 10 years old. That morning I woke up eager to work on my volcano project with my Uncle Tim, Dad's brother. My father was a politician of some note, considered the father of multi-party democracy in Liberia.

When Liberia's civil war started in 1989, he was instrumental in bringing peacekeeping troops to Liberia as rebels overran the capital city. Rebel leaders tried to take the country by force and did not like the fact they had been stopped just short of their goal. As a top diplomat, he believed in finding peaceful solutions and protecting innocent lives. This day would be a test of that. Rebel forces, disguised as protesters, used children in the crowds. These unknowing children were meant to be used as human shields and cover for the rebel soldiers. First, they attacked my father's office a few miles away. A security person at the office frantically radioed that the crowd was on their way to our home. I stood by nervously, quietly hoping the report was wrong.

"Maybe they'll decide not to come here," I thought to myself.

A few minutes later, I could hear them chanting in the distance. As the noise grew louder, I became increasingly nervous. My stomach felt queasy, wondering what would happen next. A large crowd arrived at our front gate. My father, flanked by two bodyguards, Mac Howard and another man, walked towards them to speak with the group. He said a few words, and that is when they attacked, throwing large rocks at us. I was on the porch when it started. Someone told me to run back inside. I went into my Dad's bedroom to look out the window, and that's when I heard a massive BOOM!! It was the sound of a grenade exploding in our front yard. A piece of shrapnel hit and cracked the glass. I ran back out, thinking we might need to flee. One of the bodyguards was holding an AK-47 pointed at the mob.

"Don't shoot at them! Shoot in the air!" My father yelled repeatedly. Those words will always stay with me. When we would have been fully justified in using deadly force to defend our home during that attack, my father saw

the children. I saw them too. Some were my age. We ran towards the back of the house, away from the mob, some of whom were carrying guns. One of our bodyguards, Augustine, was hit in the neck by shrapnel. I noticed blood dripping from his body. He leaned against the wall, leaving a bloody trail as he slumped down to the ground. We climbed over the back fence. It was deafening and chaotic as we tried to escape. A small group of bodyguards tried to get my father away, but the mob realized we had fled through the back and started coming after us. I stood there, looking around, thinking about what to do next. Suddenly another bodyguard, Tom Diggs, grabbed me by the hand and started leading me away. A few minutes later, a group of men armed with rocks and large sticks surrounded Tom and me.

"That's one of them!" one of the men yelled.

"I don't know what you're talking about," Tom replied unconvincingly.

At that moment, I expected that my life was about to end at ten years old. I figured they would attack Tom first, and I'd be next. Just when I thought they were about to strike; my father and a few bodyguards came around the corner. I'll never forget the look on my father's face at that moment. He looked at me with fearful concern and then noticed Tom with me. The men surrounding us quickly ran after him forcing them to turn back around. Tom grabbed my hand, and we took off running.

I looked to my left and noticed a girl around my age on her porch. She yelled, "Catch him!" and let out a sneering laugh. Did she realize he was someone's father? Did she know they were trying to kill or hurt him? I wanted to say something to her, but I couldn't. We had just been spared and needed to get out of there. Tom took me to his home nearby and locked me in a room. I was terrified. Did someone see us, I wondered. What if someone followed us? I'd have no escape. Fortunately, no one followed us.

Tom Diggs saved my life that day. They overran our home, damaged it inside, and even set our two cars on fire. We later learned it was a coordinated attack on six prominent people's homes. We were the only ones overran but were the only ones where no one was killed. Augustine survived, so did Koffa, who was hit in the head with a rock and needed emergency surgery on his skull. We later learned that a rock or screwdriver hit our father's ear, leading to some injury. This was not the first, nor the last time we would nearly get killed or seriously hurt during our childhood in Liberia."

Eyewitness testimonial by Martin Matthews

In the 1990s, Liberia was at war with herself. Brief moments of "peace" were regularly rudely interjected by brutal conflict, leaving hundreds of thousands internally displaced or seeking refuge, with tens of thousands murdered, raped, maimed, and marred. It was a period when your last name and ethnicity were enough to get you killed. As the children of the political newsmakers, it was a time when you were a sure target.

Having a father like Gabriel Baccus Matthews meant many things; first and foremost, it meant being born into and daily surrounded by the rarefied air of Liberia's political struggles. Throughout his life, my father's relationship with Liberia was complicated. They were like two inseparable, young lovers, smitten by unbridled passion. It was love, sometimes sensual, sometimes frustrating, sometimes misunderstood, yet so riveting it would lead them down a path, where for all the devotion they felt for each other, their consummate union was never to be. Here are my recollections of that day's events...

It was Saturday, January 14th, 1995, in Monrovia. The day began like most days at that time of the year, it was months into the dry season, and the sun made its presence felt across the blue, equatorial sky. That Saturday, as we often did, Mom and I got dressed to head over to Grandma's on Jamaica Road, Bushrod Island. We took rice, oil, and other food items as we always did and would check up on my younger brother Jehu, the youngest of us, who was literally Grandma's baby and lived there with her from the age of two years. Grandma had lost her son, Uncle Junior, during the 1990 episode of the war; Jehu had come as a timely consolation.

Not wanting my mother to get ready before I did, I hurriedly dress up, gulp down my tea, and rush to wait in the car. The drive to Jamaica Road was the same as it had been countless times before. The usual traffic lined up along the road as people hustled and bustled through the streets of Monrovia. Traffic police whistled and controlled movement as street hawkers went about their business, ever watchful for the next customer. It was a typical Saturday morning in Monrovia; except for my family, as I would soon find out, this day would prove to be an unforgettable one. Our house was attacked while Mom and I were at Grandma's. Our cars were set ablaze, grenades exploded in our front yard, with Dad, my brothers, and several bodyguards all nearly losing their lives. My brothers had to jump the fence to make it to safety; Dad had to find his way to the nearest enclave of ECOMOG[e] peacekeepers.

---

e ECOMOG: Established in August 1990, ECOMOG, the Economic Community of West African States Monitoring Group is a West African multilateral armed force mandated by the Economic Community of West African States (ECOWAS), made up of soldiers from the national armies of member nations to help keep the peace and re-establish stability within the sub-region.

I was only 7 years old at the time; still, I will never forget the gruesome image of Dad's bloody ear or the long recovery of the guards who had to be medevacked to South Africa for urgent medical attention. My mother and I were not there at the time, but the trauma of just how quickly our entire world could come crashing down would stay with me for years to come. Most people erroneously identify the life of a politician's family in Africa as one of fame, fortune, and connections; yet, much comes with the package of our famous parents that is often overlooked.

***

My father, Gabriel Baccus Matthews, stepped onto the stage of Liberian history in the 1970s. After schooling in the US at the City University of New York in Political Science and working briefly with the Liberian Consulate, he returned to Liberia. Young and audacious, he was drawn into national issues even as a student. His involvement in grassroots politics in Liberia was quite the paradox. Dad was born to an Americo-Liberian father from Virginia's up-river settlement in Montserrado county and a mother of native ancestry from Sinoe and Rivercess counties.

Along with like-minded idealists, in 1974, he established the Progressive Alliance of Liberia (PAL), the first legal opposition party to be recognized in Liberia in decades of single-party rule. PAL later morphed into the Progressive People's Party (PPP) and subsequently became the United People's Party (UPP). In April 1979, Dad, along with other Progressives of his time, protested the increase in the price of rice, the nation's staple, from US$22 to US$30 per 50kg bag. The April 14th Rice Riots, as they would come to be known, would mark a turning point in Liberia's 132-year history. Former President Ellen Johnson-Sirleaf describes the riots as follows:

"The riots proved, once and for all, that the society had been radicalized. There was no turning away from that fact, no putting the genie back into the bottle[17]."

By the time I came along in the late 1980s, Dad had been knee-deep in the trenches of Liberian politics for well over a decade. He had gone from being a leading opposition player in the late 1970s to a government official in the early 1980s and then back into opposition by the end of the decade. So, it comes as no surprise that, as his daughter, I grew up eclipsed by Liberia's political struggles. Politics was not a job for Dad; it was a calling. A passion. He helped establish a well-oiled political machine that mobilized massive grassroots support, produced publications, and emerged as a significant player in a country that had, since the 1870s, come to know only one dominant political party—the True Whig Party (TWP). From his youth until his dying day, politics would define everything in and around his life—including ours.

Growing up, we spent our mornings at school and afternoons at the UPP party headquarters on the Old Road while our parents attended yet another strategic planning meeting. By the time I was 12, I had a basic knowledge of diplomacy, understood different political persuasions, had listened in on the drafting of speeches and sat in the shadows of countless interviews. I had seen what it took to plan a political rally, the mobilization involved, the meticulous planning, gathering, discussing, lobbying, and canvassing that had to precede a successful single-day event. And who could ever forget the battle cries? My goodness! I get goosebumps just remembering:

"Bartee, oh Bartee!!! Bartee oh Bartee!!!!!" was the crescendo that accompanied the mantra,

"In the cause of the people, the struggle continues."

By my 16th birthday, I had been on campaign trails, attended more political rallies, met more dignitaries, and knew more about Thomas Sankara, Julius Nyerere, and Kwame Nkrumah than any other teenager. I learned all this by merely watching and listening. From birth, I had been enrolled in a masterclass on grassroots politics. Politics was a part of my life without me realizing it. I saw it all and, with child-like curiosity, soaked it all in without any conscious thought.

My mother, Helena Teta Ajavon, was just as passionate and very in step with the politics of the times. A member of PAL, Mom, was arrested along with Dad and several others following the infamous rice riots. She was taken in as a political prisoner to the notorious Post Stockade Prison. The riot leaders, Dad, and 13 others were charged with sedition. They were later granted amnesty after an independent investigation into the day's events but not before being stripped, starved, repeatedly flogged, and daily tortured with abrasive cowhide that lacerated the skin off their backs[18]. Many of his fellow prisoners recount how Dad altruistically took daily beatings for several of the other prisoners. The scars on his back and extensive dermatitis on his forearms decades later were evidence of the torture and filth he endured during his prison days.

A few of us his children, born much later in the 80s, have similar traces of eczema and hyperpigmentation on our forearms, a legacy to that dark era. The prison rashes were so pronounced they found their way through the gene pool. Whenever I ask my mother to share her recollections as a political prisoner during those times, with a pained gaze and an eagerness to change the topic, she rarely recounts those horrific weeks of uncertainty in the Post Stockade. Mom's usually very vivid and chatty by nature; on this topic, her words are always few.

Despite the apparent dangers and grave sacrifices, Mom was fully vested in the change process. With her remarkable people skills and jovial nature, she helped rally the women, organized fundraising events for the party, and patiently met with the tens of people who showed up at our house each day, all longing to be heard. Apart from the party headquarters, our house was a central meeting ground for people who wanted a personal audience with Dad. Tens of people would show up, seven days a week, as early as daylight, for various reasons, hoping to have Dad help them solve one problem or the other. Mom made it a point to ensure they had transportation and something to eat before leaving. My mother's personality has always been warm and inviting, making her a natural people magnet. Coupled with her striking Arabian beauty, people of all walks of life gravitate to her. She gets along so well with people and readily finds a family where others would see perfect strangers.

Back in the 80s and 90s, Mom was a skilled entrepreneur and educator; she owned several businesses, including Ayorkor's Furniture Center, named after me, and St. Martin's Commercial Institute, in honor of my brother Martin. Founded in 1986, St. Martin's Commercial Institute was a reputable learning institution that trained thousands of graduates in management, secretarial science, and bookkeeping. It remained operational until Liberia's second civil war in 2003 when the premise was utterly vandalized, and Mom finally lost the will-power to start over, having done so countless times before. From the 1970s to now, Mom maintains a keen interest in politics and closely follows current events as they unfold across the media. Her favorite cable news program host is Rachel Maddow; that should tell you just how much she remains engaged.

It was an interesting dynamic, being raised by two

passionately driven people whose daily pursuits centered around a singular purpose: multi-party democracy and social justice for all Liberians. Our values and worldviews were profoundly shaped by our parents' vision for a more democratically inclusive Liberia.

Meanwhile, throughout Liberia's extended crisis, as "Baccus Matthews' children," our lives would continuously be at risk. From the 1970s, when Dad was wanted dead or alive, to the insurgencies in 1989, 1992, 1995, 1996, and 2003, our safety always seemed fluid. It was a lot to absorb in one's childhood. There were times we had to abruptly go into hiding, not knowing where our father was, or even if he was okay, spend the night huddled together in the pouring rain on the beach, or escape home with nothing more than the clothes we had on. Martin even had to wear a few of my dresses at one point; whenever the single pair of jeans he managed to escape with would have to be washed.

In all these instances, families risked their lives, opened their homes and hearts, shared their food and space at tremendous personal risk to keep us safe and alive. My family will always be indebted to these many people; my siblings and I owe our lives and survival to you. In all our many close calls, a few grievous memories linger.

The first is when my brothers escaped home and found their way to New Kru Town at Mr. Kollie's home with his family. Mr. Kollie[f] had been a longtime party sympathizer and a friend of Dad's. He had two wives, one of whom had recently given birth to twins. The boys would be safe there overnight, or so they thought.

That night, something was amiss in the atmosphere. My younger brother, Tony, got up to pee. Drunk with sleep, he walked sluggishly through the narrow hallway to the

f Not his real name.

bathroom when a shadow aiming a gun in his direction appeared on the adjacent moonlit wall. Ameria[g], Mr. Kollie's nursing wife, still awake from breastfeeding moments before, jumped into motion, briskly pushing Tony to safety in the open doorway as the bullets sprayed her chest and lower abdomen. She fell to her knees, feebly whispering:

"Run, Tony, run! You boys need to run."

Tony is alive today because Mrs. Kollie sacrificed her life to save his. She died inches away from him. Two innocent, beautiful children went through life without their birth mother because one brave woman could not watch another's child die. I sob each time I recollect that somber night.

Then there was the night at the onset of the April 6th, 1996 crisis. I was spending the Easter holidays at Grandma's when the unrest began. Jehu and I were the only Matthews siblings there at the time. It was a night like many others— low key, quiet, and indoors. During the day, Jehu and I would spend most of the day inside, avoiding being seen by passersby. Jamaica Road was the main shortcut to Logan Town, New Kru Town, and other parts of Bushrod Island from Somalia Drive.

As tensions escalated, hundreds began plying the streets, escaping to safety. Since you never know who might be in the crowd that would recognize us, Grandma made sure we stayed indoors. You see, that's the thing about war; once the shooting starts, people follow their basic survival instinct, and flee, many times, not knowing exactly where they are going. They pack up their essential belongings, round up their kids, and off they go. The plan crystallizes along the way.

So many people would pass through Jamaica Road onto

---

g Not her real name.

their next destination, wherever that would be. The idea of being near the Freeport of Monrovia was also a pseudo-guarantee of daily access to food. Those staying closer to the coveted harbor had access to more sustainable food supplies and other necessities during past conflicts than those living further away, hence the rush to Bushrod Island. The road would stay busy throughout the day and, thanks to the nationwide curfew being enforced by the peacekeepers, would become misty quiet at night.

One evening, after we had all retired to our various sleeping corners after family devotion, the silence was broken when a pickup truck rudely drove into the yard. There were no cars on the streets this late except for peacekeepers and rebels. It did not sound like this car came in peace.

Several armed boys—some as little as age 10, jumped out of the moving pickup and began firing recklessly into the air. "Where the Baccuh Mafew chirren weh here[h]?" My bladder nearly let loose. Lying flat on the floor, I began shaking in fear; my cousin Adolphus crawled over, motioning to me to lie still and keep quiet.

"Where the Baccuh Mafew Ma weh geh this house? Leh her come ohssah with the chirren na or we will burn the damn thing, na na![i]"

"Oh God! Oh God! Oh God!" I repeatedly whispered, drenched in sweat from fear and the multiple layers of clothing I had on. Each night before sleeping, I would wear a pair of shorts and a tank top, long trousers, and a t-shirt, beneath a knee-length dress and an old pair of sneakers that I seemed to be outgrowing. The rationale for the multi-layers was that if we ever had to make a run for it, I would get out with more than just one article of clothing.

---

h "Where are Baccus Matthews children?"
i "Where is Baccus Matthews' Mom who owns this house? Have her come out with the kids or else we will set the house on fire!"

Grandma bravely stood to her feet and headed for the door.

"Oh God, we are gonna die! We are all gonna die!" I scream to myself. I was scared stiff, afraid Own Mama would be killed, and we would all follow. I silently recited the 23rd Psalm,

"Ye though I walk through the valley of the shadow of death, I will feee---aaaar!!!"

More shots fired; this time, it's right under the window.

By then, Grandma opened the front door and stepped into the moonlight.

"I yeh! I yeh. Who looking for me? See me yeh na. You ask for Baccuh Mafew Ma? Yeh me yeh.[j]"

Grandma was my Mother's mom, but in this context, as far as these guys were concerned, Mom, Mom-in-law, God-mother whatever—it was the same thing. They didn't care for details.

The leader spoke up, "Where Baccuh Mafew chiren? Leh allor yor come ohsah yeh.[k]"

"Wehtin yor want do with my chiren? I myseh yeh, no need for chiren. Anything yor want do to me, yor do it! Yor already killed my other son during the 1990 war. Yor can come for me but, yor will never go near my grandchiren!![l]"

By then, I had nearly lost it! The tears started rolling down my cheeks. Adolphus crawled over and placed one sweaty palm over my mouth, "Shhhhh...." He repeatedly said.

---

j "I am here. I am here. Who's looking for me? You asked for Baccus Matthews mom, here I am."

k Where are the Matthews children? All of you should come out here."

l "What do you want with my grandchildren? You have me, there is no need for my children. You rebels already killed my other son during the 1990 war. You can come for me but you will never go near my grandchildren!"

"Ok, my Oldma^m, I hear you. I will think about it, but what you got here to eat? I hear say you luh be feeding people at your house here."

Just then, a second car drove into the yard. Another tall figure furiously stepped out, slamming the door shut.

"Who the hell told your to stop here?" He shouted.

"Who sent your on Jamaica Road? I told your to patrol the area, not to go harassing people!"

It was Aloysius. Aloysius had grown up on Jamaica Road. Like my cousins Adolphus and Eddie, his father, too, had been killed in the 1990 episode of the war. His mother and Grandma were staunch Catholics; they often attended church events at the same Parish. Aloysius would spend many days in our compound, eating and hanging out with my older cousins. Shocking the pervasive effects the war had on Liberia's youth and children. "When did he join the rebel forces?" I wondered. Recognizing Grandma outside in the moonlight, he quickly rebuked them:

"Who the hell told your to harass my Oldma? Who the hell sent your here?"

With fire in his eyes, he directed his loaded gun at the relaxed child soldiers, who had now made themselves comfortable on our back porch, waiting eagerly to be fed.

"Get your asses out of here now, before I finish somebody!"

Turning to Grandma, Aloysius knelt, pleadingly holding her feet, "Own Mama, I am so sorry! I am so sorry. Please forgive them. They didn't know the house. It will never happen again."

---

m Oldma, terminology used as sign of respect to refer to an older woman in Liberian culture.

"It's ok, Aloysius. It's ok. They didn't know. Since they are hungry, I will prepare something for the children. We have to let the children eat." Affectionately known as everyone's Ma, "Own Mama," Grandma set out to prepare food for the group.

And that is how that deadly situation was quelled. Own Mama stepped into the house, rallying everyone to help cook rice with palm oil and canned sardines for them, while the boys, mainly child soldiers, sprawled on our back porch, smoked weed and chatted in the moonlight. I could not bring myself to help or eat; I was much too traumatized from the near-death experience just moments before.

***

In his historical anthology, *Scary Dreams*, recounting his own childhood in conflict, Liberian Poet Lekpele M. Nyamalon writes:

> *"May generations after us come and read that children growing up in conflict can also tell their stories, no matter how faint, in some way, they too can put a dot in the lines of a story of how conflicts affect their lives[19]."*

Growing up surrounded by such trauma, if there is one thing I learned, it is this: politics is a) a matter of perspective, b) fueled by the side of the fence on which a person and his/her ancestry sit, and c) if they chose to sit on the fence with indifference. Several years after the conflict ended, Liberian Nobel laureate Leymah Gbowee, in her unforgettable 172nd Liberia Independence Day oration, in 2019, would weigh in on this notion by categorizing Liberia's political ideologies as the "the Ruling Position," "the Opposition," and "the No Position." Madame Gbowee concluded her audacious address by proffering a pathway to reconciliation:

"When the groups are separated and scattered from one another, we are unable to work together to meet our common goals. We cannot be coordinated, and we move in opposite directions from one another. (....) When the three groups come together in service of our nation, we will have true peace."[20]

Interestingly, when the war in Liberia finally ended in 2003, it did not matter which "position" a person found him/herself in over the years. Everyone, "Country" or "Congo," rich or poor, educated or uneducated, in one way or the other, had been directly affected by the carnage and chaos meted out during the nation's decade and a half of civil war.

When it was all said and done, we were all losers with a cloak of loss closely trailing us each day of our lives—lost innocence, lost dreams, lost families, lost relations, lost status, lost homes, lost progress. Every single Liberian had lost something and some part of themselves as a result of the senseless war.

***

Chapter 2

Growing Up Matthews

"Sunsets, like childhood, are viewed with wonder not just because they are beautiful, but because they are fleeting[21]."

Richard Paul Evans, Author

When I peel away the gruesome, blood-stained layers from my childhood, I can still recall a few pleasant memories on the fringes of chaos. I remember the mouth-watering aroma of Grandma's freshly baked cornbread laid out to cool in a tray. A house full of wide-eyed, growing bellies all lined up in anticipation of the first slice. Long breaks from school over at Own Mama's on Bushrod Island was something we looked forward to during our growing years. We got to meet up with cousins we saw only a few times during the school year and squeeze ourselves into every nook and cranny of Grandma's house for several weeks. Her heart-warming homemade shortbread, donuts, and leftovers would quickly replace the tea and bread staple we had on bustling school mornings back at home.

While there, we would indulge in endless games of hopscotch, "touch," "knock foot," and jump-rope competitions while cooking, cleaning, and doing other chores around the house. We would wind down the day fetching water for our evening baths, playing a few games of cards and ludo, and take turns at telling "make-believe" spider and scary stories under the cool, outdoor moonlight in the backyard.

With much of Liberia's electricity and water infrastructure destroyed during the war, a daily chore was to fetch household water from the wells or handpumps several blocks away. This would be used for bathing and cooking. We also collected what little tap water came flowing that day since tap water was believed to be safer than well water for drinking. The water pressure from the war-ravaged White Plains Water Treatment Plant was inadequate to supply, but a few liters each day. Thus, collected tap water, a rare commodity, was reserved only for drinking. These early life experiences—queuing at wells, carrying heavy water containers overhead, pushing jerrycans in metallic wheelbarrows over several blocks—would be the fuel driving my later career choice in the budding field of water, sanitation, and hygiene (WASH). In the 21st century, this experience remains the unfortunate daily reality for millions of children worldwide.

At Grandma's, I got to hang out with my childhood buddies Dekontee and Charlotte; we took turns playing at each other's house. Having been raised among boys, I enjoyed hanging out with girls my age, playing house, and pretending to cook lavish meals from discarded ingredients and onion peels we mixed and mashed into empty tomato cans from Grandma's kitchen.

At the end of the break, there was always a sense of sadness leading up to our return home; but for me, that feeling would quickly dissipate, making room for back-to-school excitement. Ever the nerd, I could not wait to don my starched, gold shirt and pleated navy-blue skirt—elementary uniform of the J. J. Roberts United Methodist School. School, libraries, and books have been some of my favorite places and things since childhood. I sailed through Mrs. Swen's 3rd grade class, landing on the Principal's Special Student list. By the end of the year, I was awarded a double promotion to the 5th grade. My parents beamed with pride; the after-school study sessions were paying off immensely.

My 5th grade year would end up being cut short, with several months left to go. On April 6th, 1996, relations between the warlords—now all headquartered in Monrovia thanks to another power-sharing deal, took a downward spiral, plunging the country into another episode of brutal conflict. In no time, we found ourselves internally displaced, at the ECOMOG Base at St. Paul Bridge, with other families of current and former Government officials. Hundreds of us slept in the officers' mess hall, and with limited bathroom facilities for the displaced crowd, we found ourselves bathing while dark and having to poo out in the open yard. This, too, would later influence my passion for humanitarian and development work in sub-Saharan Africa.

Several months later, as things stabilized and schools reopened, I started my 6th grade journey. Sixth grade was when I met one of the best teachers ever, Mrs. Susannah Zunnah. Mrs. Zunnah, as we called her, was a headteacher for one of J.J. Roberts' three Grade 6 classes at the time; she taught Biology. She had characteristic sleepy eyes and was one of the softest spoken yet firm instructors I ever had. She taught with a passion and knew her stuff in and out. Her attention to detail and command of her subject matter quickly piqued my interest in the natural sciences.

Suddenly, Biology was not just something you memorized; it was something you understood. There was a synergistic rationale to form and function, a logic to biological design. That was the year I first began courting the idea of a career in the natural sciences, all thanks to Mrs. Zunnah. Life would take its course, and I would not return to J. J. Roberts for another seven years, reuniting with my beloved teacher for just one final semester in my senior year of high school.

***

In 1997, Liberia held its first elections since its descent into civil war in December 1989. I was 10 years old at the time, too young to fully comprehend the historical ramifications of the events unfolding around me but old enough to realize that they were significant. Dad was one of 13 candidates contesting in the race, so that meant we were in the thick of all the campaigning and electioneering. The daily crowd at our house tripled; the political meetings doubled, and everywhere we turned, someone was wearing a white t-shirt with Dad's picture and the green United People's Party logo emblazoned across their chest. People came and went throughout the day and late into the night, meeting, mobilizing, and canvassing. The battle cries were an all-day constant. The atmosphere was so palpable, it could not be escaped.

Following the 1996 clashes, security was beefed up for each of the presidential aspirants as a precaution—many of whom were former warlords-turned-aspirants. Officers from the Liberia National Police and peacekeepers from the West African mediating force, ECOMOG, were assigned to Dad to cover close-body protection. We went about our normal school activities, and on weekends, we would accompany Dad to events. My older brothers had the chance to join the campaign trail across Liberia, getting a full view of the nation—memories they continue to cherish. Whether we understood it or not, history was being made, and in some form, we had an opportunity to witness it firsthand.

That year, former warlord Charles Taylor shocked the world by winning Liberia's first post-war polls with a massive 75.3 percent of votes[22]. It would be the second time in Liberia's recent history that democratic elections were being held, which included a broader ethnic representation.

Mom, my siblings and I moved to Abidjan shortly after that. Some of my fondest childhood memories stem from my teenage years growing up with my brothers in neighboring Abidjan, la Côte d'Ivoire. Our school, Jin-A School, was owned by a Franco-German couple, the Elias family, with their kids enrolled in the program. With a Christian curriculum and international affiliations, Jin-A quickly became the cosmopolitan, melting pot school. You could find everyone from Liberia's newly elected President Charles Taylor's daughter, Charlene, to his Vice President, Enoch Dogolea's six kids, to students from the US, Congo, South Korea, Rwanda, Taiwan, and France.

Mbalu Sankoh, daughter of Foday Sankoh, Sierra Leone's Revolutionary United Front (RUF) leader, also attended Jin-A. The first and only time I would see Sankoh in person was in Jin-A's courtyard, during a visit to his daughter. Not much taller than I was, he looked quite different from the Captain Hook-like villain my 11-year-old mind had pictured a rebel leader would be. Cautious, I watched from afar as Mbalu rushed to hug her father. It was a tough scene for my best friend, Mariama, from Sierra Leone, who also attended Jin-A. Mariama's father, a renowned Medical Doctor, had been taken captive by RUF rebels for many years and was being held behind rebel lines. With her Dad held hostage, she, her mom, and sisters were forced to live a hard, uncertain life in exile in Abidjan, unsure their father would ever make it out alive.

Madam Lorette Elias and her husband ran a correspondence program modeled after the Christian Liberty Academy Satellite School System in Arlington Heights, USA. They did their best to offer a holistic learning experience. Sports classes were on Mondays, music and piano lessons during the week, while swimming classes, by far everyone's favorite, were on Thursdays at *Club House Le Vallon in Deux Plateaux*. We had French lessons daily to ensure we gained fluency in Cote d'Ivoire's official language. The teachers were of diverse nationalities—Ivorian, Nigerian, Liberian, and the Caribbean. In Jin-A, I learned to swim, play a few notes on the piano, develop French fluency, and became immersed in literary classics. Those were the good old days when all we had to do was study, keep up good grades, do our chores, and be teenagers.

Abidjan holds a special place in my heart because it was the only period in our lives as siblings when five of us, Jerry, Martin, Andrew, Tony, and I all attended the same school. When we weren't studying, we would spend our free time playing PlayStation PS1 FIFA 98 and Street Fighter II Plus Alpha video games. A tomboy at heart, I had learned to play video games from very early on. We each had different interests, and how we spent our money was a reflection of that. The older siblings saved what little allowance our parents gave us for good behavior to take girls out on dates. Andrew, ever the music fan, saved his cash to get newly released CDs. Back then, Tony was more interested in junk food and baggy jeans. Having hit puberty, I would buy female essentials and, of course, books. All through my life, bookstores and libraries have been my happy place, so you can imagine how much time I spent in the *La Librairie de France* bookstore. I would lose track of time, tucked in a snug corner, leafing through classics.

When it comes to cuisine, French pastry sits in a class of its own, and the Ivorian capital was one place you could get the best *baguettes*, croissants, *pains au chocolat,* and *quiches*. With France's strong influence on local fashion and haute couture, Abidjan's tailors were among the best I ever had. They were creative geniuses at designing dazzling outfits from African fabrics.

As a person who has come to attach much value to faith and family, beyond my parents' instrumentality, Abidjan was also where I consciously joined a church family and began paying keen attention to my Christian faith. Mom and I started attending the Bethel World Outreach Church in *Plateau Dokui* and were there every time the doors opened. In a new country, Bethel Abidjan quickly became our religious community and family away from home. The congregation was predominantly Liberian, with services translated into English and French, making room for a diverse membership from western, eastern, and central Africa.

Over time, I would volunteer as one of the church's bilingual translators and become incredibly involved in the Sunday school and youth-related activities. Reverend Jervis Witherspoon, the current Chief of Protocol, Republic of Liberia, was the General Overseer of Bethel Abidjan back then. His sermons were so electrifying and empowering; it was refreshing to hear him minister every time. His daughter, Jerlyn, a year younger than me, and I would become fast friends, a relationship we fondly maintain to this day.

Bethel Abidjan was a blend of Liberians of different ethnicities and socio-economics who had fled Liberia during the war, or following the 1997 elections, like us, seeking refuge. Many had made homes for themselves and had fully settled in la Côte d'Ivoire, hoping for a chance to enroll in the US Refugee Resettlement Program[23]. The program provided Liberian refugees opportunities to migrate and start life anew in the United States, especially during Liberia's protracted civil crisis. Prominent Liberian leaders, passing through Abidjan, always made it a point to stop by and fellowship at Bethel.

Apart from her public appearances during Liberia's 1997 elections, the first time I saw Ellen Johnson-Sirleaf up close was at a service in Bethel Abidjan. From time to time, she would show up with her teenage grandson, Stephen Sirleaf, holding a silver cane and seemingly resting much of her weight on his young shoulders. She appeared ill and frail at the time, impossible to predict from merely looking at her then that this same woman would become the first elected female President on the African continent in less than a decade. Destiny is such a powerful thing; as we say in Liberia, *"what's for you will surely see your face."* I guess Ma Ellen's life is proof of that.

For all its charms, Abidjan was also where I lived through my first coup d'etat. Born seven years after Liberia's 1980 coup, the 1999 upheaval in Côte d'Ivoire would be my first point of reference for a political occurrence that had sadly become incredibly commonplace on the continent.

It was Christmas Eve 1999, and Dad was visiting us for the holidays. We all watched TV in the house as a family and shared light-hearted laughs when, suddenly, we heard scattered gunshots in the distance. Given la Côte d'Ivoire's reputation for peace since its independence in 1960, coupled with the season's festivities, it could only be fireworks, I first thought. As the shooting intensified, we soon realized we were living through a hostile takeover.

A few hours later, the regular TV broadcast was interrupted. An older man we had never seen before appeared on the screen, impeccably dressed in full military fatigue, flanked by armed soldiers. President Henri Konan Bédié, in power since 1993 after succeeding the nation's beloved founding father, Félix Houphouët-Boigny, had been overthrown. The quinquagenarian gracing our screens was now the man in control of state power.

Former Army General Robert Gueï had been called out of retirement by the coup plotters to head a transitional government, *le Comité National de Salut Public[n],* which was expected to lead the country up to elections. His famous *"Nous sommes venus pour balayer[o]"* post-coup television address is one I remember vividly to this day. For several years after the 1999 coup, la Côte d'Ivoire, like its eastern neighbor, Liberia, would face its own geopolitical challenges, eventually plunging into a deadly conflict. Years after the coup, ethnic and tribal tensions continued to rise in Abidjan. At school, I would sometimes hear my Ivorian classmates discussing politics, naïvely arguing among themselves along ethnic lines:

"Well, if it's a war they want, it's a war they will get."

When you have never lived through shelling and shooting, it's tempting to see civil war as a solution. But when you have survived a bloody childhood, lived through the terror of multiple near-death experiences, it is an experience you would never wish upon your worst enemy. It would take a dozen years of conflict, recurring coup attempts, and a massive economic downturn before la Cote d'Ivoire would finally take a turn back towards full stability.

---

n The National Public Salvation Committee (1999-2000)
o "We have come to sweep."

My teenage years in Abidjan were also a period of growth and character development for me. It was the first time I consciously decided to color outside the lines. In 10th grade, I decided to switch schools from Jin-A, where I had been doing so well academically, to something intensely more challenging. I decided to trade in my English-speaking Jin-A School curriculum to enroll at *Collège International Lemania,* where the medium of instruction would be entirely in French. My parents were apprehensive about my bold move at the start of senior high, but I was very decisive even as a 14-year-old. Leaving the familiarity of schooling in my first language to immerse myself in an environment where I would be forced to stretch the limits of my bilingual skills was scary. Still, I decided to take on the task. I was determined to maintain excellent grades even though every single course would be taught in French. As resolute as I was, my first week was a disaster. Every teacher threw pop quizzes at us that I could have readily aced in English but struggled to get through in standard French. I refused to give up.

If there is one thing that experience taught me about myself, it is this: Maggie gets it done. No matter how hard, how daunting, or how much sleep it will cost, Maggie will get it done. It was a rough switch, but I had made up my mind to put in the work. Thanks to my parents, I got a tutor for each course, putting in several hours after school into one-on-one sessions. For the next three years, I attended summer school to be ahead of the class each September. I put aside all my favorite books in English and began reading everything in French, from the Bible to the newspaper, Shakespeare, to comic books. By the end of that school year, not only was I first in the class, I ranked in the top 5 in French Grammar, Spelling, and Composition. Twenty years later, my French is still as good as my English. I speak, read, and write both languages fluently.

Meanwhile, hundreds of miles from Liberia, the dynamics of our nation's history would continue to come into play in my childhood. It was one bittersweet reality that came with being a Matthews, which I was not quite prepared for. One Sunday afternoon after church, I tagged along with a friend to a mutual friend's birthday party at this lovely home, which belonged to a Liberian family in Abidjan. Like the other teenagers, I made friends and had a good time playing games, eating, and dancing. Everything was going on so well until this tall, middle-aged woman decided to ask the infamous "whose child are you" questions Liberian adults tend to ask.

"This little girl can dance! You are so cute! And would you look at all that hair! What's your name?" She asked while running her long, ruby-red fingertips through my luscious ponytail.

Blushing at the compliment, I respond a shy, "My name is Magdalene."

"Magdalene, who?" She adds.

"Magdalene Matthews." I beam with a smile.

Her facial expression and body language immediately change from pleasant to hostile:

"Which Matthews is that?"

Everything in me would wish that this lovely woman was one of the moderates that would be polite enough to mask their disdain, but 8 times out of 10, the reaction would be the same. My reply, "Baccus Matthews," would be met with a snarl and sometimes a shove. Some would demand I no longer associate with their kids because my father had, in their words, "spoiled the country" and now had the nerve to parade his children around theirs.

I would often go home in tears, bewildered by this newfound animosity towards me. I knew of Liberia's divisive sociological constructs from elementary school social studies. Still, it wasn't until I began having such experiences that I began to fully grasp the extent and impact of Dad's role in confronting the status quo. My brother, Gabriel, who grew up in the 70s in the heat of Dad's activism, often shares the complexities of his childhood, navigating these waters, as most of his friends, classmates, and relations were from prominent Americo-Liberian families.

Back to Leymah Gbowee's categories, how we were received at any given time would depend on which "position" a person's ancestry occupied relative to Dad's politics. If they were indigenous, we were hailed; if not, we were scorned. Growing up in Liberia surrounded by UPP sympathizers, in a cocoon of like-minded people who admired and respected my father, never once had it occurred to me until Abidjan that there would be people who'd despise me merely because of whose daughter I was. I remember asking Dad, one day,

"Why do they hate me so? I never did anything to them! I was not even born when you got into politics! What does any of this have to do with me? I only wanted to be friends with her daughter."

That's when my parents had to give me "the talk." Remember the uncomfortable conversation about race that most African-American parents must have with their kids to prepare them for life outside their walls? My parents had to have the dreaded "Americo-Liberian/Indigenous talk" with us early on to better equip us to navigate situations with people who would not necessarily welcome us with open arms. Initially, I misread their reaction as a rejection of my person; I later learned that it had nothing to do with me. It was all predicated on just one thing—whose daughter I was. I was the target they could reach.

As with all situations in life, some individuals were very crude. Yet, many others had chosen to grow past the century-long divide, seeing themselves as "ministers of reconciliation.[24]" These would open their homes and hearts to me, teaching me a valuable life lesson. They taught me that reconciliation, harmony, tolerance, coexistence are profoundly personal decisions.

While we may collectively aspire for a more cohesive national unity, the individual's role in that intricate puzzle cannot be underestimated. I learned that it takes individuals intent on *"moving beyond past wounds and hurts and building a culture of respect, dignity, and flowering love[25]"* to establish a national culture of healing and reconciliation. As Nelson Mandela said:

> *"We must strive to be moved by a generosity of spirit that will enable us to outgrow the hatred and conflicts of the past[26]."*

***

As diverse as my childhood experiences were, so was the style of parenting I was raised with. I would live with my mother for the first 12 years of my life, then with my stepmother, Miss P, for the next four, and lastly, with Grandma into adulthood. This allowed me to glean insights from different generations, cultures, perspectives, and outlooks on life. During all these transitions, one thing remained constant: Dad. No matter where we were or who our primary caregiver was, Dad would be a continuous presence in our lives, influencing everything from what we wore, the places we went to the schools we attended.

As we affectionately call her, Miss P, my stepmom, is originally Jamaican; she later naturalized as a Liberian. She was kind to us and remains a loving source of support even now. Later in life, my mom would marry a nice fellow she met during her high school days at Tubman High. Uncle Joe would come to play a significant role in my adult life as a wise sounding-board and awesome grandpa to the kids. In a way, you can say I was blessed to glean wisdom and guidance from two sets of mothers and fathers throughout my life.

While I managed the changes as best as I could at those different stages of life, to be honest, growing up for the most part of my formative years without my mother was one of the most challenging hurdles of my life. Now that I am older and a mother myself, I better understand the precarious conditions that life sometimes presents. Mom and I have delightfully grown immensely closer in recent years, in a fabulous friendship that continues to blossom.

Mom relocated to the US in the heat of the 2003 Liberian conflict; still, she made a point to be present for all of my life's pivotal moments. She was there to lend comfort during Dad's funeral in 2007 and made sure to spread her lappa[p] in proud celebration at my college graduation two years later. Mom held my hand as I prepared to march down the aisle on my wedding day, dressed to kill in her royal blue, Mother of the Bride gown, and buttercup gold hat. She's played an integral role in helping me pursue my dreams and in welcoming and caring for my kids. Back in grad school, she would post canned palm butter[q] to me

p Lappa: African waist scarf
q Ingredients for "palm nut soup" the West African delicacy, or as we call it in Liberia "palm butter"

halfway across the globe to ensure I had African food over the Christmas holidays.

My mother, Helena Teta Ajavon, is one heck of a strong woman. She has lived through a lot, from politics to prison, war, displacement, the loss of loved ones, and having to start life over many times. Life did not always deal her its best hand of cards, yet she's graciously played the hand she was dealt. Each day, watching her ebullience is a gift; she is strength personified, heart unfeigned, and soul unleashed. She embodies a zest for life, a youthful exuberance, deep care for others, and a sense of humor that has kept me going through the changing scenes of life, even while miles away.

Growing up Matthews was not a journey for the fainthearted, but if I had a choice in another lifetime, I would still choose to be a Matthews. I would not have it any other way. When it's all said and done, it is the blood coursing through my veins and the fiery passion that burns in my bones. Precisely because of who I am and the extraordinary family I was born into, my life has been a masterclass in resilience, a lesson in humility, and a reminder to maximize moments.

My teenage years taught me to be unafraid of kings but fully aware of the ordinary guy in the shadows and the need to address both with respect. I learned to see people as people, not for what they own, drive, or wear but for the simplistic authenticity of who they are as individuals. Life taught me that the people who would come to your aid in near-death situations may have no formal education, own no riches, nor possess any of the vain things we tend to think are so essential. Yet, when it would matter most, they would be the most loyal ones by your side. So, how you treat all people really does matter.

My unconventional upbringing awoke a consciousness that I continue to take with me to the hand pumps in

Sanniquellie, Liberia, during water testing and into the schools and health facilities in Moroto, Uganda, during assessments. That ability to recognize and respect another's condition, genuinely desire to help, and meaningfully contribute, for me, is one of the greatest blessings and burdens of being a Matthews.

Living through violent unrest in Liberia, coup d'état, and eventual conflict in Côte d'Ivoire coupled with sociological interactions with people of different persuasions taught me many things. I learned that where politics is about choosing sides, national reconciliation is a matter of individual choice. A person decides to forgive, let go and move past a given situation—to reconcile. When many of us make that decision, national reconciliation then becomes possible.

I am of the firm belief that despite our checkered past, Liberia can reconcile. The country can heal and move past the multiple historical antecedents that ushered us to where we are now. National reconciliation and healing are possible. But it will require individual decisions from every Liberian to a) move beyond the pains of our past, b) intentionally pursue emotional and psycho-social healing, and c) consciously give our children a more conciliated future—one which transcends socio-economic, geo-political, or ethnic divides.

Chapter 3

In the Shadow of Politics

"and when all the wars are over, a butterfly will still be beautiful[27]."
Ruskin Bond, Author, and Novelist

Many books have been written by athletes, entrepreneurs, innovators, world leaders, and politicians. Very few accounts and recollections have been penned from the perspective of the children of politicians and leaders. I find this to be true even more of the children of leaders in Africa—these silent but fascinating eyewitnesses to history's unfolding. As the daughter of one of Liberia's leading political figures, what did it mean really to live in the shadow of politics? If I were to summarize my experience as a politician's child in Africa, I would list four things:

a) Having to live up to certain unrealistic ideals to be a good example,

b) Being the object of constant scrutiny and living a life of limited privacy;

c) Being subject to extremes: excessive bullying or hailing, admiration, or rejection;

d) Being expected to know, support, defend, and eventually carry on your parents' legacy, regardless of how old, learned, interested, or prepared you are.

You can choose many things in life, yet no one gets to choose their parents and the choices they make concerning their career paths and political persuasions. And while we have little to no say in it, as politicians' kids and family members, we end up going along for the ride our entire lives. Michelle Obama, in *Becoming,* narrates her experience of life in the quagmire of political machinery. Having her every statement, appearance, and gesture weighed and assessed, scrutinized, and criticized. Appearing in the most low-key, least expected areas and still being recognized by someone for whose wife, daughter, or son you are.

In the US, it is considered politically incorrect to go after politicians' children, especially minors. In Liberia and other parts of Africa, no such rule exists. Politicians and their children are all fair game. In fact, a politician's ability to deliver is often considered directly proportional to how scandal-free his/her kids are. It is believed that if you cannot control your kids and manage your family, the smallest microcosm of society, you are consequently not fit to lead the nation.

As a result, political children wound up as collateral damage in the political machinery of the time, fully exposed to their parents' decision-making vices and virtues. Just a few hours binge-watching episodes from the TV Show "Madam Secretary" would provide great insights on this. Better still, one season of the Nigerian Netflix Series "Sons of the Caliphate" should be all the masterclass you need to see how these dynamics interplay in the African context.

Depending on where your famous parents sit on the fence, whether "in position" or "opposition," there is also a mix of fear and insecurity—a terrifying realization that you could be a walking target of verbal and physical harm should they step on the wrong toes. During my Dad's active political years, I was still very young, but my exposure would not allow my mind to be. I had read enough, seen enough, and knew enough about Liberia's history to know that politics could be deadly. When my budding curiosity questioned Dad why he was so deeply ingrained into politics, his answer was simple. With his father's passing when he was still a little boy, Dad had grown up heavily influenced by his mother, Rebecca, and both of his grandmothers. On his father's side, his grandmother was of the establishment.

Daughter of former President James Spriggs Payne, my great-Grandmother, Georgia Payne Cooper, was the Secretary of the Liberian Senate and known to be the fastest typist in the Upper House. Her family was Americo-Liberian, influential, and closely related either by parentage or marriage to Liberia's ruling families. On the other hand, Dad's mother's Mom was indigenous, of the Bassa tribe, from Moweh District in Rivercess County. She had little education and had never before seen an electric lightbulb.

Dad recalled how he would spend holidays at both grandmothers' homes, leaving very troubled by the stark contrast—a memory that would stick with him for life. He would soon grow up to realize that he represented the intersection of the nation's two social classes; he embodied the juncture where the two roads met. Meanwhile, the older I got and experienced how dangerous Dad's involvement in Liberian politics was—especially after attacks on our home—my young, selfish mind would sometimes wish he had just left the "people's thing" alone.

"Anyone else could have done it; why did it have to be you? Why **YOU?**" I'd tearfully ask him.

To which he'd reply: "Korkor, we are striving to make sure, Ma Grace, Old Man Zio, Pa Alfred, and all these people you see here each day, get to send their children to good schools, have good hospitals, safe water, electricity and be able to work good jobs. That's why."

I did not fully grasp the concepts of equality and social justice back then. Yet, as French novelist Victor Hugo would say, *"Nothing is more powerful than an idea whose time has come[28]."* With democratic ideals gaining foothold across the now-independent, former British and French colonies in Africa, the time had come for steadier democratic inclusion in Liberia, the continent's oldest independent Republic. Everyone's voice, regardless of ethnicity and origin, had to count on the platform of social justice. Not everyone can look the other way; I guess Dad was one of them.

People have come to attribute multiple rationales to Baccus Matthews' actions over the years. As his children—censured to life in the thick of his activism, we were firsthand witnesses to the sincerity of his motives. Dad would often sit in the living room at night, in silence, alone with his thoughts, strategizing on ways to help transform the nation into a more equitable society. He loved Liberia—he loved her deeply. Dad did not just lead people; he cared for them. He took them along. So many times, he would sacrifice what should have been our tuition, our rent, and our food money to help people pay theirs instead.

He remembered names, faces and took a keen interest in the lives of the countless people who showed up at our house each day. He listened to them, inspired them, and encouraged them to keep going, despite the persistent challenges. He had a way of connecting with people across socio-economic barriers. He could be intellectual and prim and proper when he had to be, and in the next breath, down to earth and approachable to the market woman's concerns.

Thanks to his mother's formidable upbringing, Dad was religious in his values; he spoke the Bassa language fluently and connected with people on a deeply personal level. Conversations were filled with empathy for the present, bold visions for the future, interspersed with light-hearted humor.

With time, I discovered that another shortfall of being political children is that you run the risk of never being identified as individuals no matter what you achieve or become your entire life. Like appendages, you are seen as mere extensions of your famous parents. You end up perceived by a predefined scale that seems to apply only to the children of the brave men and women who venture into political waters. The closest analogy that comes to mind is being the child of a celebrated singer or athlete. Everyone holds their breath, waiting and watching to see just how well you put your famous genes to use. "Son or daughter of" becomes your claim to fame.

In 2012, I wrote and released my first book, *RISE! Redeeming the Future of Liberia, a Practical Guide to Self-Development*. I had spent months researching and working on the content while fully engaged in graduate school. *RISE!* is a contextualized self-help and nation-building resource I am pleased to have contributed to Liberia's literary and youth empowerment scene.

Interestingly, the day after the book launch, the newspaper headlines simply read, *"Baccus Daughter Launches Book."* One had to comb through several lines of the article before my name was even mentioned.

For all the cons, being the child of a politician is not without its pros. On the flip side, the prominent people who turned up at my book launch, for example, probably would not have, had I not been "Baccus' daughter."

Despite our effacing individuality, as politicians' children, it's essential to know and appreciate that our parents' shoulders are the ones on which we stand. Their achievements and legacy—however kind history chooses to be to them, are the foundations we build upon.

***

Liberia, 2003

Upon reflection, most people can easily recall the moment of their coming of age—that monumental milestone in which they went from being a timid child into a budding adult. The cues are purely biological for the butterfly when it makes that historical transition from a silent, stationary chrysalis into a beautiful, eye-catching, winged creature. For the millions of girls forced into child marriage in many parts of the world each year, it is, sadly, the arrival of their first period. For some of my college schoolmates, it was when they left home for the very first time to attend school, thousands of miles away. For me, it was the year I turned 16.

After several memorable years in Abidjan, in January 2003, just 2 months shy of my 16th birthday, my parents saw it fit to move me back to Liberia. La Cote d'Ivoire was now having major political issues of her own. Since the 1999 coup and onset of civil war in 2001, things had grown very shaky across the country. Interestingly, I was also being followed. With no extended relations in Abidjan, when a supposed "uncle" of mine showed up on my campus to ask of me after school one day, that was the final straw. Dad had me moved back home to Liberia in the middle of my senior year of high school.

Finishing high school in Liberia was a drastic shift for me. I went from studying all subjects in French, including

Literature, Philosophy, Calculus, and Ivorian Geography, back to Algebra, Geometry, and Liberian History. After forcing my brain to process complex information in one language for nearly three years, I now had to switch back to English. It was a weird move back to the familiar.

I was both excited and apprehensive at being back home. I had to settle back into my old neighborhood and make new friends in a familiar place, yet so different, recognizable, yet strange. So much had changed in Liberia since I had left six years before. The climate, the people, and the places were pretty much the same, yet altered. We still lived in the same house, a stone-throw away from the smaller James Spriggs Payne Airport in Sinkor, but everything about the atmosphere seemed different.

My old school, J.J. Roberts United Methodist, had evolved from just a Junior High, with 9th grade graduates, to a full-fledged Senior High School with 10-12th graders and graduates heading straight to college. Old classmates from elementary were now high school seniors, driving to school, owning cell phones during a time when owning one was considered a status symbol, and sporting designer handbags to school in addition to their usual bookbags.

Still growing out of my teenage tomboy streak, this was all new to me. The school's strict dress code rules from years before had been eased, allowing female students more liberty with hairstyles and lip-gloss. Many of my close friends had relocated following the April 6, 1996 episode of the war. Other schoolmates had evolved with time, now saying "hi" from a distance.

It would take several weeks before I would make friends and somewhat settle in. With a few classmates owning cars and dating older men, there was a lot of peer pressure. Sex was an unspoken expectation in any relationship, and the boys could be pretty fast and touchy, very unlike the timid Ivorian boys back in Abidjan. It was a very new environment that I naively tried to navigate. Somehow, I managed to sail through my final semester of high school unscathed, focusing more on school and my grades.

By nature, I tend to be a planner. Ever the high-achiever, I have an aversion to uncertainty. I tend to like to have my next steps carefully mapped out. Like a chess game, I try to foresee my next 2-3 moves on the board of life. I use this as a compass to keep me motivated about the future. I remember being incredibly young when I came across the Chinese Proverb, which says:

> "The best time to plant a tree was 20 years ago. The second-best time is now[29]."

I told myself no matter the "tree" I wanted to plant with my life, I would have to be intentional from the word go. So, as early as junior high, I had developed my little roadmap for the direction my life was to follow. In my simple mind, I had planned to be done with high school at 16, obtain a Bachelor's in Biology by 20, and graduate from a world-renown medical school, preferably Johns Hopkins, by age 24. I would miraculously get married by 25 and be done having kids by 30, leaving much room to do a residency and potential Cardiology specialization.

Back then, I was fascinated by the heart's anatomy; the next stop could only be a pre-med program leading up to Cardiothoracic surgery. With such lofty dreams, I dedicated much time and attention to producing excellent results.

Life's disappointments had not yet set in to mar whatever bashful hopes I had for the future. Little did I know that my well-laid plans would be thrown out the window in just a matter of a few months. I would be facing a bleeding

Liberia.

***

I kicked off my final semester of high school on a high note. In 2003, President Charles Taylor was approaching the 5th year of his 6-year term in office; his presidency would soon be cut short due to rebel insurgency in different parts of the country. The uprisings were led by two newly formed rebel factions, the Liberians United for Reconciliation and Democracy (LURD) and the Movement for Democracy in Liberia (MODEL), invading Liberia from different locations, limiting the peace mainly to the capital, Monrovia. From 1999 to 2003, LURD and MODEL forces would inch their way closer to the seat of power. Together, they would mount continued deadly attacks across the country, controlling more than half of Liberia by 2003. This would later result in President Taylor's resignation on August 11, 2003, and eventual exile in Nigeria.

By June that year, the rebels had reached Monrovia. Things rapidly escalated, forcing the international community to step in, calling for peace talks in Ghana. With mediation from the Economic Community of West African States (ECOWAS), peace talks began on June 4, 2003, in the Ghanaian capital, Accra, marking the first-time warring factions would meet since the insurgency started in 1999[30]. Former Nigerian President Abdulsalami Abubakar served as Chief Mediator.

President Charles Taylor arrived in Ghana on the first day of the talks to attend the opening ceremony. To the shock of the world, including the host government, David Crane, Chief Prosecutor of the Special Court for Sierra Leone, issued a warrant for President Taylor's arrest for his alleged involvement in Sierra Leone's own decade-long civil conflict[31]. Taylor's presence in Ghana was seen as an opportunity to apprehend him.

I remember that Wednesday so vividly because, within hours, things got so tense in Monrovia, Mom and I had to go into hiding at a relative's house on Camp Johnson Road. The entire country was on edge. People were glued to their radios, closely following developments as they unfolded.

Everyone held their breaths when the BBC[r] announced that the arrest warrant for Liberia's sitting President had been served on Ghana's authorities and transmitted to Interpol. Then Ghanaian President, John Kufuor, was the presiding Chair of ECOWAS; current President Nana Akuffo-Addo was Ghana's Foreign Minister at the time.

In Liberia, we had no idea if the Ghanaian authorities would comply and arrest President Taylor or not; what we were sure of was the chaotic outcome it would cause in Monrovia. Within moments of the announcement, the Director of Taylor's Special Security Service (SSS), General Benjamin Yeaten, took to the airwaves to caution that there would be "military vibrations" if President Taylor were to be arrested on foreign soil. Things went south rather quickly after that.

The US Government, always a step ahead in intelligence, began reaching out to its citizens, signaling possible evacuation. The US Embassy phoned my mother, informing her of the need to ensure that my younger brother Jehu, a US citizen, was safe and accessible, should they need to evacuate. Jehu still lived with Grandma, so we alerted her to prepare to leave in case things worsened.

With the stunt move the Chief Prosecutor pulled in Ghana, things deteriorated faster than anyone could imagine. The shelling intensified; the rebels, resolute in their advancement, insisted there would be no peace deals unless Charles Taylor stepped down. The Liberian peace talks lost

---

r British Broadcasting Corporation

steam, as participants, in the cozy serenity of Ghana's M Plaza Hotel, turned their attention to other things.

Nobel Laureate Leymah Gbowee, present in Ghana at the time, protesting for peace along with other women outside the talks in Accra, shares this account in *Mighty Be Our Powers*[32]:

> *"There was no resolution to the negotiations in sight. The descriptions of the stalemate were always the same: the talks are stalled; the talks are at an impasse. Meanwhile, the men of LURD and MODEL woke up every morning in their ocean-view hotel rooms, went downstairs to breakfast, and then to sessions that appeared to be completely, outrageously useless. In the off-hours, you could observe these self-satisfied negotiators lounging around the hotel pool in crisp new shirts, having drinks."*

Although the talks stalled in Ghana, the fighting in Liberia intensified. By June 7[th,] 2003, a convoy of US Marines arrived at our house, requesting citizen Jehu Matthews. They drove into our yard in full combat gear. A jeep gunner sat on guard atop a heavily loaded machine gun, ready for anything at any moment.

Down with a severe bout of malaria, I was not strong enough to face the perils of another civil conflict, but I had no choice. The rebels were approaching. We had to act fast. Mom and I hurriedly climbed into our car and drove in between the two Marine corps jeeps at high speed to pick up Jehu and Grandma. The massive chaos downtown was evidence of just how quickly things had gone south. Countless people lined the streets, fleeing with belongings on their heads and children on their backs—a scene of escape that was now all too familiar. We drove past the Freeport of Monrovia, a coveted target in all of Liberia's wars. Government fighters in pickup trucks went on past, gazing viciously at the Marines; the Marines returned the menacing glare. I could only pray they knew better than to engage these highly trained, combat-ready US Marines. Terrified, I nervously swallow. Sweat beads moisten my hairline. I say a silent prayer.

As we turned off Somalia Drive and onto Jamaica Road, immediately, we saw him. One of Charles Taylor's men, whom we all recognized. He carried two enormous machine guns, one strapped on each arm, the metallic rounds draping around him like a vest. He pointed the barrel of one weapon at a guy who was kneeling, pleadingly, before him. My mother let out a horrified gasp and rushed to cover my eyes, hoping to shield me from seeing a man possibly get shot in broad daylight. Seeing the Marines, he hesitated, repositioned himself, watching intently as we drove on past, onto the dirt road leading into Grandma's driveway.

Grandma was packed and ready to go by the time we got there. The plan was to see them off to the embassy in Mamba Point. And so, we drove back across the Gabriel Tucker Bridge, through Rock Town, and onto Mamba Point, to the US Embassy. In Liberia, the US Embassy overlooks the Atlantic Ocean, giving them the tactical advantage of amphibious missions. Combat-ready Marines stood on guard above the perimeter walls, armed to their teeth. I had driven past the embassy countless times before, but never in a time of crisis. The sheer military might on display atop the buildings was intimidating. We said our teary goodbyes as Jehu and Grandma crossed the street to the front gate leading to Consular Services, where other US families had now gathered. Mom went along to make sure they were processed. Grandma and Jehu entered the embassy, Mom and I returned home.

Several hours later that evening, we received another

call. The Embassy Officer alerted Mom that after careful review of Jehu's travel arrangements, they could not authorize Grandma's evacuation. No documents attested to Grandma's legal guardianship of Jehu; his mother would have to accompany him instead. Moments later, the Marines were back. Mom was noticeably confused. Dad was away in Ghana, attending the Liberian peace talks; he had left his phone, and since he last called us the day before, we had no way of reaching him now to glean from his wisdom. Grandma not being able to go was not part of the plan.

"Ayorkor will stay with the Oldma until things settle," Mom said, voicing her muddled thoughts.

The Marine leading the convoy kept glancing at his watch, nudging Mom to hurry. Perplexed, she kept going in and out of the house, trying to pack her travel essentials. Having had to escape countless times before, Mom had gathered all our passports in one place, in case of emergency.

"Ma'am, we have approximately 3 minutes to head back to Base."

She made more calls, trying to figure out what to do next. Mom went into her room once more. By then, time was up.

"I am sorry, Ma'am, but we have to leave now. I have my orders to get you to safety as quickly as possible. We have to leave right away."

And so, just like that, amid an uprising, our family split up. On Monday, June 9, 2003, under Operation Shining Express[33], Mom and Jehu left for the US as part of nearly 500 people, including 100 Americans, embassy personnel, and 29 international UN staff members evacuated by French helicopters from the US Embassy and European Union compounds in Mamba Point[34].

I was left with a very inconsolable Grandma who, heartbroken over my brother's departure, opted to leave our house and head to an Aunt's place on the Old Road. A few hours later, she was gone. With all the adults gone, I was left alone at home with my foster sister Hawa, who wasn't much older than me, my younger brother Tony and the few security guards, Pa Dolo and Ramsey George, who managed to stay despite the growing conflict.

With Mom gone and the rebels closing in on Monrovia, my options grew slimmer by the day. Dad had called to confirm his safe arrival in Accra much earlier, but we had not heard from him since. I knew he was safe, of that much, I was sure, but I had no means of contacting him.

The shelling grew louder each day, signaling the advancing invasion. Our house's window glasses clattered to the floor from the increased vibrations. We were quickly running out of food. I was still being treated at home for malaria by a family friend nurse who lived nearby. With both parents unreachable, I had no idea what to do next. Never had I found myself so vulnerable, so exposed in a crisis, with neither of my folks around for guidance.

I had to figure out the next steps on my own.

Our house was being surveilled. Different cars kept stopping by, at all hours of the day, with several people, some government, some rebel affiliates, checking on Dad's whereabouts. His decision to quietly sneak out days before to attend the peace talks in Ghana was paying off.

Our house was easily visible behind the low-lying, 4-foot-tall white-washed fence. These guys would drive in, glance around, and try to peep through open curtains to assess who all were in the house. I stayed indoors, away from the windows, and kept my head down. Efforts to broker a speedy peace agreement between President Charles Taylor's government and the invading LURD and MODEL rebel forces dragged along in Ghana. The resulting tensions continued to rise, and violent clashes ensued in Liberia. Things were set to get much worse before getting any better.

One afternoon, two amputee government soldiers rushed into our compound through the low-lying side gate and decided to camp out in our backyard. They were armed, high, and hungry, demanding we give them food to eat. One had a small pistol, the other, a gigantic c-shaped knife.

"So, the Papay[s] not yeh, ehn? We came to collect small thing from him[t]," one said to Pa Dolo, our aged security guard. Handicapped former combatants had a habit of showing up at prominent Liberians' homes to solicit money to get the basics—food, soap, and supplies. However, more times than not, that money ended up being used on cheap, locally brewed alcohol.

Then, spotting me through my bedroom window, with a grimace, he shouted:

"Anyway, it awreh. We na want anything from the house. Give us the papay's daughter."

I gasped, terrified as I imagined what these two blood-thirsty men had in mind for me. One thing became clear: I had to get out of there fast. It was rumored that an order had been issued days before commanding all Taylor government soldiers, amputees included, to report to duty at the frontlines to counter the invading LURD and MODEL rebel forces. But with one having a single arm and the other on crutches with a single leg, these two were definitely in no hurry to head to battle. They chose to hideout in our backyard instead.

The longer they stayed, the more horrified I became. I had

---

s Papay, terminology used as sign of respect to refer to an older man in Liberian culture.
t "So, Mr. Matthews is not here? We came by to ask him for some cash."

to get out. With sweaty palms and shaky hands, I did the bravest thing I had ever done in my 16 years alive: I picked up Dad's blue 33.10 Nokia phone, scrolled through his contacts, and phoned President Charles Taylor.

By then, I had run out of options. If anyone had the power and resources to trace and contact my Dad, it would be him.

The phone rings a few times.

I listen in for an aide or a bodyguard. With all that is going on, they sure must be busy, I thought. I let the phone ring a few more times, then reluctantly decide to hang up.

That is when I hear: "Baccus, what a surprise! To what do I owe the call?"

I froze, the deep voice unmistakable. To be honest, I did not expect him to answer. Overcome by the sheer terror of escape, not once had I reflected on what I would say when I did have Charles Taylor on the phone. I just desperately needed to reach my Dad for guidance on what to do next; I hadn't thought anything through. I had hoped to first speak to a personal assistant or so and work my way up. Of course, with a call coming in from Dad's number in an unfolding crisis, he'd answer directly. Adrenaline comes in very handy at such times.

"Hello, Mr. Pres- President," I nervously stutter, struggling to find my voice.

"Mr. President, my name is Magdalene Matthews. I am Baccus Matthews' daughter. My father is attending the peace talks in Accra, and I have been unable to reach him. My mother also is away. A lot is going on, and I'm quite concerned about my safety. Is there any way you can please assist in helping me get in touch with my Dad? I urgently need to reach him."

He listened keenly, then replied, "Just a moment."

"Does anyone of you know a certain Magdalene Matthews?" I hear him ask.

Several female voices in the background answer, "Oh yes, she's Baccus Matthews' daughter. I know her."

"She's in our school," another adds.

Liberia is a relatively small country where everyone knows each other through one social circle or the other. At the time, several of President Taylor's relations and wards attended my high school, J.J. Roberts, so verifying who I was, was not difficult.

"Ok, Magdalene, I have not spoken to your father, but I can make a few calls to see if someone has. Can you find your way to White Flower?"

Situated along Tubman Boulevard, Liberia's main suburban road, President Taylor's illustrious White Flower mansion was in Congo Town, a suburb about half an hour away.

I responded hesitantly, "Yes, Mr. President."

"Ok, Magdalene, see you in a few minutes."

With that, he was gone.

Stunned, I couldn't believe what had just happened. I had just had a direct phone conversation with the President of Liberia. If I made it through to Dad, I could get guidance on what to do, but that left one major problem? How do I leave the house without drawing attention from the intoxicated, trigger-happy amputee soldiers in our backyard?

Our security, Ramsey George, had to create a diversion. Our car was having repair issues that required taking it to Blo, our mechanic, up the street. We made sure the amputees ate, smoked, and watched the driver take the car to the mechanic several times that day, establishing a pattern. By the supposed fourth test-drive trip to the mechanic, Ramsey snuck me out through our house's side door into the trunk of our jeep. I lay flat on the floor as we quickly drove off.

The drive through the streets of Monrovia was terrifying. Leaving my house for the first time since Mom left days before, I realized the gunshots and mortar fire were much louder and a lot closer. The rebels were gaining ground, inching towards the city center. More people were walking in the streets, fleeing the violence. I grew more terrified with each passing minute.

Entering White Flower, President Taylor's residence was like stepping into another world. The serenity of the compound was a stark contrast to the chaos just outside. The security was airtight. I was carefully searched, and told mobile phones were not allowed. A bodyguard escorted me from the gate to the part of the vast, opulent compound where President Taylor was sitting. It was my first time seeing him up close. His remarkable features were even more striking in person. He was sitting a few meters away from a putti fountain, discussing intently with another prominent Liberian businessman and associate of his, whom I recognized. They chatted lightly about the elaborate fountain, which seemed to still be under construction.

Standing before President Charles Ghankay Taylor was deeply intimidating. He commanded such an indomitable presence that I felt like a dwarf, stepping impishly towards him.

"Well, hello, Magdalene. Welcome, welcome. Hope you had

no trouble getting here?" He asked.

"Please have a seat."

I smile and nod sheepishly. "How are you?" He went on.

What was I to say? The country was descending into chaos. I was recovering from malaria, scared, traumatized, unable to reach either of my parents, my house was being surveilled, and with armed amputees in my backyard, I feared for my life. The words wouldn't come. Instead, I formed a weak smile and carefully took a seat in the vacant chair across from him and his guest.

"I have made a few calls, and no one seems to know how to reach your father, Magdalene. Someone saw him at the meeting in Accra but isn't sure where he's staying."

I blink and swallow hard, still quite uneasy in my surroundings.

Can't reach Dad? My hands began to shake. "Oh, God! What do I do now?" I thought to myself. I was sure to get killed, raped, or tortured in the unfolding chaos. I tried to stay calm, fighting back terrified tears.

President Taylor motioned to a fair-skinned lady standing nearby, "Place a call to those guys again in Accra. Let's see if anyone else can reach Baccus," he instructed.

She dials a number, puts the phone on speaker for me to hear, and hands it to him. Again, no indication of where Dad was. I thanked President Taylor for his time and left.

With the rising tensions in Monrovia and Accra, I should have known Dad would conceal his whereabouts for security reasons. A seasoned opposition politician, impossible to tell a friend from a foe in such unstable times.

So here I was, unable to contact my parents, 16 years old, female, and vulnerable in a deteriorating armed conflict; the only daughter of a known opposition figure in an escalating battle with different actors and interests at stake. My life depended on quick action. I could no longer wait for instruction from my parents. War was unfolding; I didn't have the luxury of time. With the armed amputee soldiers in my backyard, the advancing rebels approaching the city, I made the quick decision to head to the airport. I had to get out of the country fast. I bought a ticket at twice the price of what it cost just days before and boarded the very last flight leaving the country for Abidjan. The very next day, all commercial flights were suspended.

The rebels overrun Monrovia.

***

I landed in a very different Abidjan from the haven it had been just months before. All Liberians arriving on flights into the country were being detained at the airport. We disembarked to join a group of hundreds of other Liberians, mostly women, some pregnant, and children held under lock and key in a particular wing of the Felix Houphouet Boigny International Airport. The Ivoirian authorities, still grappling with the aftershocks of their own civil crisis and continued internal tensions, were being extra careful in determining who was being allowed entry into their country. My fluent French and knowledge of the city, having lived there for many years, would be deciding factors in the Immigration officer's decision to let me enter the city after hours of pleading and negotiation. It would take several days for the Liberian Ambassador to reach a deal with authorities to have the other arriving passengers released from the airport.

Liberia, Sierra Leone, la Cote d'Ivoire, Guinea—from 1989, conflict in West Africa repeatedly spilled over from one country to the next, creating a cloud of instability across the entire sub-region. As things escalated in Liberia once again in 2003, the international community decided it was high time to surgically address the situation. The response was overwhelming.

By September 2003, the United Nations Security Council unanimously adopted Resolution 1509, establishing the UN Mission in Liberia (UNMIL) and deploying 15,000 military personnel, over 1000 police officers, 250 military observers, 160 staff officers, and appropriate civilian elements. It was the most substantial UN presence in any single country at the time, commanding such a leading presence, paving the way for lasting peace after a decade and a half of civil conflict.

Sadly, by the time the Liberian war finally ended in 2003, over 250,000 lives had been lost, and nearly 85 percent of the nation's infrastructure was destroyed. Families were torn apart, and the country was divided across tribal lines, the effects of which would linger for years to come. The conflict's fallouts were many: lost lives, lost families, lost property, lost youth, lost innocence, lost time, and something less spoken of—lost love.

As a result of the displacement engendered by the conflict, many people wound up marrying and raising families with partners they would have perhaps not had they not lost love. You see, love, when genuinely found, is not something you recover from quickly. All the hopes of life by the side of their chosen beloved were all squashed prematurely as lives and livelihoods were shattered, and others migrated to neighboring and distant lands to seek refuge—losing touch with the person they once so loved in the process.

My uncle met and fell in love with a charming young woman when I was a baby in the 80s. With his stunning charm and smashing diplomatic demeanor, he remains one of my favorite people in the world. Their love story would have perhaps culminated in a happy ending, but then came the Liberian conflict. Running for their lives, they ended up in different countries, and in an era where cell phones still did not exist, they lost track of each other.

As the war dragged on, they both moved on, separately finding solace and happiness in their prevailing situations, wherever they were, shutting the door on what may have been the most unforgettable love story of their lives. With time, they both learned to live and love again. Except not every love story is escapable. Some romances, like destiny, are written in the stars. The years came and went, Microsoft developed Windows, Zuckerburg conceived Facebook, and Nokia came in with the ubiquitous 33.10 mobile phone.

It took a while, but global communication was becoming a lot easier. The stars, it seems, were all lining up to give them a second chance. Thanks to technology, they were able to reconnect. Their passion was rekindled, and the reconnection was pure magic. Twenty-five years melted like wax, sparking something so strongly inevitable, they could not ignore. Seeing them together is to catch a glimpse of the unsearchable power of love. Not everyone believes in destiny. Not everyone believes in happy endings. Their love story challenges me to believe. How can I not?

I look into their mesmerized eyes, like two teenagers in love, and I am inspired. I am reminded that much beauty can emerge out of thick ashes. For all the horrors of war, lives lived out separately, their love somehow survived it all. I can't help but embrace the notion that destiny does exist, and distance, time, and geography are but minor details in the grander scheme of things. Some things are just meant to be. My uncle and aunt's love story began when I was in diapers and has stood the test of time and trials, proving that true love still exists. It is also evidence that the future is filled with immense promise if you just keep living, believing, and striving. Sooner or later, something beautiful will appear on the horizon.

So, I remain hopeful for the future of Liberia. In the optimism of US Captain Hank Bracker, Former Harbor Pilot for the Port of Monrovia,

> *"Liberia is a country on the "Pepper Coast," which in many ways mirrors the United States. While it has not been easy, the willingness of its dedicated, hardworking people has never subsided. Hopefully, their endeavor to obtain a more perfect country will continue, and perhaps the day will come when they can once again take the lead in Africa to find a brighter future[35]."*

I remain hopeful that Liberia's glorious day of renaissance will surely come in our lifetime.

SECTION 2

LOSS

Invictus

In the fell clutch of circumstance

I have not winced nor cried aloud.

Under the bludgeoning's of chance

My head is bloody but unbowed[36].

Excerpt from Invictus

William Ernest Henley, Poet

Chapter 4

Dad

"My father didn't tell me how to live.

He lived and let me watch him do it[37]."

Clarence Budington Kelland, Children's Books Author

As I look back over my life, my Dad remains the person with the single greatest influence on me as an individual. From my decision-making to my career choices, the passionate approach I bring to things, down to the attributes I looked for in the man I eventually married, his fingerprints were left on nearly every aspect of my life.

Like most girls and their fathers, Dad and I had a peculiar relationship. Out there, he was "G. Bac," "Gabe," "Baccus," "Chairman Matthews," "Minister Matthews," "Honorable Matthews," to me, he was just Dad, or "the Papay." We had much in common. We were both left-handed, talked with hand gestures, and were highly driven, passionate people. As his only daughter, I could press his buttons and bring out his incredible sense of humor.

We shared a love for all things intellectual—discussing poetry, politics, fine arts, and classic literature. Dad loved to talk, and I loved asking questions. The more I asked, the more he explained, and the more I learned so much about so many things. When it came to his political stances, Dad felt a need to ensure I always heard his side of the story and not just the media's. He would go to such lengths to make sure I understood the motives for his actions, even if I disagreed with them. He taught me that there was a back story to everything.

He went on to introduce me to Longfellow's A *Psalm of Life*, which would become one of my all-time favorite poems:

> *"Tell me not, in mournful numbers,*
> *Life is but an empty dream!*
> *For the soul is dead that slumbers,*
> *And things are not what they seem[38]."*

Indeed, things are not what they seem. Dad was a deep thinker that encouraged me to always look at things critically, finding connections and synergies where possible. We shared a love for reading and literature that would be a hallmark in our relationship, his way of teaching me about life, you could say. If he wanted to show me life lessons on ambition, he would recommend I read Shakespeare's *Macbeth*. Politics and betrayal had to be *Julius Caesar;* social inequities would be Victor Hugo's *Les Misèrables,* and strategy was Sun Tzu's *The Art of War*. From world history to politics and the arts, Dad possessed an endless wealth of knowledge, which, for me, was as inspiring as it was intimidating. He would recommend books for me to read and authors I needed to know. Dad had a memory that could effortlessly recall lengthy verses of Shakespearean plays. He pushed us for academic excellence and made sure we gave schoolwork our very best, values instilled in him by his Mom. He would tell us how he once got every single question correct on a Math test. Still, the teacher graded him 95%. Bright and early the next morning, his mother marched to school to see his teacher, demanding his remaining 5 points for an even 100%.

"Mrs. Frank, I know Gabriel did exceptionally well. But no one can be that perfect now."

Our Grandma, "Dawo," as we all affectionately call her, meaning "old lady" in the Bassa language, was not having it: "Well, Mr. Peters, this is a Math test, not essay writing. Math is very straightforward; the answer is either right or wrong. If you graded all Gabriel's answers right, there should be no reason why he should not get a perfect score. You are not here to grade a perfect individual; you are here to grade a perfect paper. If the paper is perfect, you should grade it a perfect score."

With school, passion, or politics, it was all or nothing with Dad. He encouraged us to give everything our best. Hanging out with Dad was like having a personal curriculum beyond academics, centered on broadening my worldview and preparing me for life. He would direct me to classic literature, along with works from deep thinkers like Descartes, Dante, and Locke. Then there were lengthy conversations about Thomas Sankara, Marcus Garvey, Kwame Nkrumah, Martin Luther King, Sekou Touré, and Nelson Mandela. People showed up at our house each day for different reasons, some for his help with personal problems, others to discuss politics; some came by just to hear him speak and share ideas. I cherished those enriching exchanges of ideas, history, and culture. I have always been an avid learner; those discussions would highlight topics I was eager to research further and know more about.

Then there were the regular movie nights at home watching thought pieces like *The Hunt for Red October, The Firm,*

Clear and Present Danger—all based on classics by his favorite novelists, John Grisham and Tom Clancy. Years later, I chose a career path in the sciences. Still, much of my liberal arts understanding of world history, international relations, politics, and diplomacy would be shaped from the masterclass of life spent with my Dad.

As a man, Dad was far from perfect. For all his charisma, beautiful, voluptuous women were his kryptonite, many finding his charm irresistible. At 5'11", Baccus Matthews had a cocky, confident smile, a steady gait, with shoulders that magnified his tailored suits. He was a suit-and-tie kind of guy, nearly always formally dressed and ensuring that we, too, took our appearance seriously. He was so known for showing up in suits that Grace Minor, former President of the Liberian Senate, used to jokingly say:

"Even if you invited Baccus to a beach party, he would show up in a suit."

No doubt, Baccus Matthews was a handsome man, and the ladies loved him. And like most prominent Liberian men, he would have several love interests over time. As his daughter, it was a reality I would disapprove of and confront him on, yet, regrettably had to learn to live with. Needless to say, his adventures would have lingering effects on my outlook on marriage and relationships.

As a father, Dad made sure to keep us in check. He taught us a sense of responsibility and pride in who we were as Matthews. With the dangers and challenges of life as politician' children, he made sure we looked out for each other everywhere we went. "Never lose sight of your brothers" was the #1 ground rule. As a result, we grew up as a tight-knit family. Dad had a temper that would, on rare occasions, flare up at us children, guaranteeing a spanking you were sure to remember, but that would be followed by lengthy words of wisdom that we now all appreciate. Martin shares these reflections:

"I admired my father in many ways, but he was not the "wrestle-around-with-you" type. He was a "discuss-deep-socio-political-issues" type. I quite enjoyed our conversations and time together and learned many lessons."

Dad was certainly not "the-roll-on-the-floor type" or sappy, "say-I-love-you-all-the-time type." Still, he did have his ways of expressing his affection, including a coded whistle he used to lovingly call us by. As a political activist, he was principled. His life would be driven mostly by a burden for social change, centered on creating a more just society, an "equal playing field," as he would often say. His progressive, grassroots ideologies would be the principles he would uphold to his dying day.Two of Dad's favorite quotes he'd often cite were by Otto von Bismarck, *"Politics is the art of the possible, the attainable—the art of the next best,[39]"* and Alexis de Tocqueville, *"In a democracy, the people get the government they deserve[40]."*

With his radical stances, to some, Dad was a troublemaker, an "agitator supreme[41]." Still, to many, Baccus Matthews is credited as "the "Godfather of Liberian democracy[42]," a "political Maradonna" as his followers called him, who "opened the eyes of the Liberian people," awakening an unquestionable political consciousness that would disrupt the status quo.

Dad's passionate love for Mama Liberia would be fueled by a profound commitment to her people. Take 1997. A month to the July polls, a meeting was held between ECOWAS[u] and all political leaders and aspirants—many of whom were

u The Economic Community of West African States (ECOWAS) is a regional political and economic union made up of fifteen member countries from West Africa. ECOWAS played a major mediating and peacekeeping role during the first (1989-1997) and second (1999-2003) Liberian wars.

former warlords. It would be the second time in Liberia's recent history that democratic elections were being held encompassing a broader ethnic representation. Gabriel Baccus Matthews was one of the 13 candidates contesting. The aspirants were asked to sign an undertaking to support the next President of Liberia that would emerge, regardless of who he/she might be. Each candidate, confident in their stake, eagerly signed.

When the results came in, the opposition bloc quickly fizzled, many candidates jumping ship and leaving the country. As far as Dad was concerned, he had not just signed a piece of paper to appease international observers; he had made a solemn oath to Mama Liberia, and he was going to honor it. He took the gamble to stay and help in any way he could to rebuild the country he so loved.

Edward Bulwer-Lytton once wrote: *"The pen is mightier than the sword[43]."* Not every candidate sincerely planned to live up to the implications of their pen at the Abuja meeting. Some chose to empower the sword. Shortly after, new rebel forces emerged, launching coordinated attacks that would result in the 2nd Liberian war from 1999-2003.

I remember the June 1997 Abuja meeting vividly because Martin got his first pair of glasses. He traveled with Dad to have his eyes checked and the lenses prescribed. Having done most things with my older brother growing up, I could not understand why this time was different. To quell the sibling feud, Dad took his time to explain Martin's visual issues and the meeting's focus in simple enough language for me to understand.

Depending on the year we were born, my siblings and I got to know our father in different stages of life. For Gabriel, born in the 60s, Dad was a radical revolutionary; for us, 80s babies, he was a seasoned politician, having swum through many turbulent tides throughout his career. One thing is sure, whether we liked it or not, understood it or not, were old enough to meaningfully engage in it or not, because of our father, politics was a ubiquitous part of our lives, affecting all of it.

Our lives wound up being the kind of storyline box office movies are made of. It had all the riveting ingredients—war, passion, sex, intrigue, suspense, romance, and betrayal. We had parents who had both been political prisoners in a jail they were not expected to return from. They came out and continued in the struggle. We were close enough to meet the good and bad newsmakers of the day, attend political events, and tag along on campaign trails.

Standing on the outside looking in, it was an envious life, so close to the powers that be. For us, on the inside, we knew we were born into something dangerous. We had to survive wars, face bullying from mean kids at school, tolerate rejection from the elite in society on the opposite end of Dad's politics, stay humble amid deep admiration from die-hard followers while enduring multiple near-death experiences. It was a polarized, high-stakes, pulsating existence into which we were born, but we learned a lot from it.

Our childhood was surrounded by countless people from different walks of life, contributing rich content to our worldview. Ma Grace's mobilizing energy, Mac Howard's humorous wisdom, Mary Garjay's watchful care, and visually-impaired Logan's wildly positive outlook on the future taught us so much about what's most important in life. Those everyday people in our sphere showed us respect for elders, empathy for the less fortunate, the value of people and relationships in pursuing purpose, and, most of all, the power of a single vote within a democracy, regardless of who casts it. They weren't all educated, and many had never traveled beyond their small county's jurisdiction, least of all the African continent, making Liberia all the perspective they had. Yet, in a democracy, as in life, none of that should matter. In a genuinely equitable democratic system, with a level playing field, their vote, voice, and vision should be as valid as the college graduate's. This was the herculean task my parents were striving to accomplish.

Looking back, I realize some of my fondest memories with Dad were the weeks we spent together in Accra in 2006 and 2007 as he was undergoing treatment for cancer in Ghana. I would learn many things about him, his motives, his aspirations, and his political backstory during those many weeks, just us two. For the first time in my entire life, I had my father all to myself, away from the crowds, the politics, the press, and life's pressures.

During this time, he would bequeath his side of the historical story; he would entrust me with something priceless: the words of a dying man. We would spend Christmas 2006 watching Aljazeera news, closely following Saddam Hussein's unfolding trial and then-Senator Barack Obama's rapid ascent on the American political landscape. For someone like me, whose most prominent love language is quality time, that was the best Christmas gift ever. In March 2007, we would quietly celebrate my 20th birthday, eating takeout from Celsbridge, my favorite eatery in Accra.

Another of my most memorable moments with Dad was the once-in-a-lifetime opportunity to hang on his arm and attend the historic inauguration of President Ellen Johnson-Sirleaf, Liberia's first elected female President. In October 2005, Ellen Johnson-Sirleaf ran against football legend George Weah and won, becoming the first woman President on the African continent. The inauguration was set for January 16th, 2006. Everyone who was anyone was attending. Dozens of world leaders showed up in solidarity to mark the turn of an era in Africa's oldest republic.

From US First Lady Barbara Bush and Secretary of State Condoleeza Rice, to the Presidents of Niger, Nigeria, Ghana, South Africa, Sierra Leone, Burkina Faso, Mali, and Togo. Officials of the United Nations, African Union, and ECOWAS showed up in their numbers for the momentous occasion to witness an embattled nation reborn.

I had seen Madam Sirleaf up-close several times at church in Abidjan and at political meetings, but it was clear that day would be remarkably different. In keeping with his grassroots ideologies, Dad had thrown his weight behind George Weah in the just-ended elections. Still, as a prominent political opposition figure, he was invited to the event. I was home from college in Ghana for the holidays, so he insisted I tag along as his plus one.

For weeks, work had been underway on the grounds of the Executive Mansion and the adjacent Capitol Building to create an open space large enough to accommodate the thousands of guests and citizens that would be in attendance. The sidewalks were carefully swept, the streets received a fresh coat of paint, decorators worked their magic, and carpenters worked tirelessly to build the podium. The nation's colors, red, white, and blue, jubilantly shouted from every turn.

It would be my first inauguration attended, and I could not wait for the day to come. I had carefully chosen an appropriately formal black dress, velvet heels, a cute silver clutch, and silver jewelry to match. My hair had been straightened and let loose to cascade down my shoulders. French tips, my signature nail design for formal events, had also been done days before. As far as my appearance was concerned, I was set and ready to go.

As excited as I was to attend an official function, I had not fully grasped the significance of what I was about to witness; but Dad understood the power of representation. After centuries of patriarchy, a woman was finally elected President of an African state; despite their opposing views, it was crucial to him that I, a young African woman, see that. He sought to engrave a legendary image in my subconscious. He wanted me to see just how far an African woman could reach in the 21st century. He wanted me to be proud to be a woman, an African woman, a Liberian woman. He wanted me to believe in the beauty of my dreams, despite how unattainable they seemed or who stood by in opposition. Growing up, he would always urge me to be resilient. He'd often say:

"Korkor, if you are going to succeed at anything in life, you will have to work smarter, try harder, and stick at things much longer than the boys."

He knew that society could be unkind to us girls. He'd caution that society would demand I work twice as hard to prove myself because I'm a girl. None of that made sense to me as a dreamy teenager in the sheltered confines of home— it sure does now in the corporate world. For all their political differences, Dad wanted me to know that, in the end, Ma Ellen's gender did not stop the fulfillment of her dreams. If ever I was to doubt that, I would have the palpable memory of her historic inauguration to prove otherwise. He often stressed that Liberian women should demand more than just 30% political representation because they had so much to offer posterity, morally, economically, and politically. Madame Sirleaf was to be a test of that.

Beautifully wrapped in a pearly ivory African outfit with

an auspiciously imposing head-tie, Ellen Johnson Sirleaf delivered her first address as 24th President of the Republic of Liberia:

> *"In the history of nations, each generation is summoned to define its nation's purpose and character. Now, it is our time to state clearly and unequivocally who we are, as Liberians—and where we plan to take this country in the next six years[44]."*

The 2006 Inaugural Address, later dubbed the "Papa Na Come Speech" from an analogy used during her rendering, would come to be a defining moment in the Sirleaf presidency. Thanks to Dad, I was there, watching history in the making. I learned many things that day, the loudest lesson being it is okay to be a girl. It was January 16th, 2006, the most influential person in Liberia was being sworn into office, and for the first time in 160 years, it was a SHE.

***

Dad lived a full life; he did everything intentionally, purposefully, and passionately. Whether it was in pursuit of ambition, purpose, or policies, he knew what he wanted and went after it. If asked to summarize Gabriel Baccus Matthews' most significant contribution to the course of modern Liberian history, in my view, Article 77 of the 1986 Constitution captures it succinctly. You see, the original text of the Liberian Constitution of 1847, Chapter 1, Article 11, Section 1, was abundantly clear:

> *"All elections shall be by ballot, and every male citizen, of twenty-one years of age, **possessing real estate**, shall have the right of suffrage[45]."*

The right of suffrage, i.e., the right to vote, was only accessible to **male** real estate owners. In a country where, for over 100 years, only property owners could vote, Dad's push for multi-party democracy was the bridge to inclusive participation. A right guaranteed to all regardless of gender, social status, or land ownership. With the advent of democratic pluralism, Article 77 of the 1986 text, which covers voting rights, would later read:

> *"a. Since the essence of democracy is free competition of ideas expressed by political parties and political groups as well as by individuals, parties may freely be established to advocate the political opinions of the people. Laws, regulations, decrees, or measures which might have the effect of creating a one-party state shall be declared unconstitutional.*
>
> *b. All elections shall be by secret ballot as may be determined by the Elections Commission, and **every Liberian citizen, not less than 18 years of age, shall have the right** to be registered as a voter and to vote in public elections and referenda under this Constitution. The Legislature shall enact laws indicating the category of Liberians who shall not form or become members of political parties."*

Baccus Matthews lit the match that would spark the flame of a movement for democratic pluralism after decades of mono-party rule. He ushered in an era that reintroduced democracy as a free competition of ideas expressed by multiple political parties in 20th century Liberia. Thus granting every Liberian citizen, 18 years and older, the right to vote and chose their leaders, regardless of who those leaders might be. Late US Congressman and Civil Rights icon, John Lewis, put it this way:

"The vote is precious. It is the most powerful non-violent tool we have in a democratic society, and we must use it[46]."

Yet, to use it, the vote must be accessible to all. The ethnic and gender diversity of the candidates contesting Liberia's General and Presidential Elections in 1997, 2005, 2011, and 2017 shows increased democratic inclusion in recent Liberian history. On Baccus' role in Liberian politics, as eulogized by Prelate Dr. Katurah York Cooper, she noted: "The thing speaks for itself."

As a man, an activist, and a politician, Baccus Matthews was not without fault. In fact, it was the great Nelson Mandela that said:

"In real life, we deal, not with gods, but with ordinary humans like ourselves: men and women who are full of contradictions, who are stable and fickle, strong and weak, famous and infamous[47]."

Still, the role he played in recent Liberian history can never be ignored. For all their limitations and contradictions, the Progressive Alliance of Liberia (PAL), and the wider actors of the Progressive Class of the 1970s, will be etched in time as the pioneering shoulders upon which current political movements stand. In a moving tribute, famed Liberian Journalist, Joseph Bartuah, writes:

"Like all mortal beings, Baccus was not infallible. There were times that he erred in his political activism, in terms of some public pronouncements and certain decisions he took. However, one thing is certain: even some of his staunchest critics will reluctantly concede that he was an exceptional revolutionary who played a significant role in Liberia's forward march towards the covetous culture of democratic pluralism[48]."

President Ellen Johson Sirleaf would also come to write of him:

> *"The two of us often found ourselves in contention; we did not always see eye to eye, but we both worked long and diligently to serve our native land. But by the time of his death, many decades later, I meant it when I called him the Godfather of Liberian Democracy and said he had left an indelible mark on our country's political history. Despite the many contradictions he represented, Gabriel Baccus Matthews will be remembered as one of Liberia's greatest sons[49]."*

As children of a man driving a cause, we had to accept to share our father every day of our lives—with his people, his purpose, his passions, and his politics. His fatherly counsel, seasoned wisdom, and political acumen would extend to many throughout his life. He was our father, but he was never ours alone. In 2007, at age 59, after a battle with cancer, Dad died in the arms of the Liberia he so loved. His weeklong burial, too, would include both quiet family and traffic-stopping public ceremonies, again making room for the many who needed to pay their last respects.

Of course, I longed to have had my father around much longer, to share his wisdom on my writings, to cheer me on at my graduations, to march me down the aisle, to meet his bubbly grandkids. Yet, for however long we had him, he left indelible footprints in our hearts and in the sands of time.

As African legend, Chinua Achebe once said,

> *"Until the lions have their historians, the history of the hunt will always glorify the hunter[50]."*

History will remember Baccus Matthews based on who the storyteller is. Depending on which side of Liberia's geopolitical divide a person's ancestry found itself during Baccus Matthews' active years, the story will be told from a different vantage point. But with the hard-won introduction of universal suffrage, Baccus Matthews secured a seat at the decision-making table for all Liberians irrespective of social class. For better or worse, objectively, that is what he will be most remembered by. In his own words at the 2002 National Peace and Reconciliation Conference:

"Ladies and Gentlemen, there is no permanence in nature. King Solomon, in his wisdom, is said to have given a ring to the chief architect of the Temple of Jerusalem when work began on that monumental edifice. The ring bore the inscription, "This, too, shall pass away." By the late 1970s, it was clear that change had become an inevitable necessity. Change had to come to make reconciliation possible. I today call on all Liberians to reconcile themselves to the inevitability of change. To everything under the sun, there is a season.

Change was coming. Identify all the advocates and actors you may. Blame or applaud whichever ones you wish; change was coming. It was coming, whether the names of the actors were Baccus Matthews, William R. Tolbert, Jr., Richard Henries, Samuel Doe, Joseph Chesson, Thomas Quiwonkpa, Amos Sawyer, Togba Nah Tipoteh, Boima Fahnbulleh, Oscar Quiah, Rev. Toimu Reeves, Bishop George Browne, Father Michael Francis, etc., change was coming. It was coming with them, without them, or even in spite of them. It was coming, and it came. God is always on time. Liberia had to be saved for all of us, and not just for some of us. And our generation succeeded in bringing us together. Yes, we do see what you see, and we should all seek to contain what is wrong. In time, however, the dust will settle, and a clear stream will replace the muddy waters[51]."

What he managed to accomplish in his life and nation will be recorded in Liberian history for generations to come, leaving his children and followers as the custodians of that legacy. As divergent as the views may be, one thing is certain, for all his imperfections, Gabriel Baccus Matthews' legacy in the history of Mama Liberia will remain forged in the crucible of time.

Chapter 5

Shattered Glass

There's a history of heartbreak,

Tucked in the creases of her eyes,

A museum of the moments,

That she'd watched just pass her by,

And each tear that escaped her,

Held the things she'd left unsaid,

So the words she'd never spoken,

Stained her dampened cheeks instead[52].

e.h

Liberia, 2004

It was January 2004, several months after the end of the Second Liberian Civil War. Life seemed to be returning to normal as best as it could. After a few months in Abidjan, I returned home to Monrovia towards the end of the year. I still recall where I was at midnight on December 31st, 2003, ringing in the New Year. Like thousands of other grateful Liberians around the country, I was in church, dancing and clapping my way into 2004, at the annual New Year's Eve Watch Night Service at the Bethel Cathedral of Hope in Congo Town. The praise and worship session was electric. After months running for our lives, escaping shelling, living through displacement, and near starvation the year before, those who survived were profoundly thankful to be alive.

As the clock struck 12:00, everyone broke into a dance, jubilating and hugging each other as Pastor Wolo M. Belleh—now Bishop, Head Prelate of Bethel Monrovia, pronounced blessings for the months ahead. The year seemed to indeed be jetting off to a great start.

A month later, I was at home cleaning my parents' bedroom when Pa Dolo, our elderly watchman, came running in with his brown, portable battery-powered FM radio. The Liberia Chapter of the governing West African Examination Council (WAEC) had just released the official results of the 12th grade WAEC exams administered the year before.

"Magdalene Matthews! Magdalene Matthews! They just called your name on the radio, Ayorkor. They say you topped WAEC! You topped WAEC exams in the whole country. Listen, Listen."

Pa Dolo cranked up the volume. The announcer went on:

> *"This is a special congratulatory treat to Ms. Magdalene Matthews of the J.J. Roberts United Methodist School for your Division 1 success on the 2003 WAEC exams. Ms. Matthews had the highest aggregate score, Division 1 results in the national exams. Congratulations, Magdalene, Liberia is proud of you."*

I was stunned. It was my first time hearing my name on the radio for something other than clichéd birthday shoutouts. A small crowd of people who had been waiting outside to meet with Dad that day chased Pa Dolo into the house, and all began hugging and congratulating me. The older women began spreading their lappas for me to walk on, a traditional sign of honor. My younger brother Tony, who was now in his junior year, came rushing in and, between peals of laughter, tossed my slender teenage frame in the air:

"You did it, Korkor!" I giggled in disbelief, reality still sinking.

As the highest scorer nationwide in the 2003 West African Exams in Liberia, I was later told I qualified for a government scholarship. However, the powers that be would choose to play politics with the hopes of a 17-year-old girl. The National Transitional Government of Liberia was now running the country in the lead up to general and presidential elections in 2005. The Government's firm commitment morphed from a guaranteed scholarship to a promise of a US$5,000 token support towards my education. Either way, I was grateful.

I was phoned into the Ministry of Finance to collect the cheque. After several weeks of giving me the run-around, putting me through the tedious flights of stairs to the 6th floor, asthma inhaler in hand—the MOF's elevator was out of service at the time—it became apparent things were never meant to materialize.

One day, after waiting for hours in the office of the Finance Ministry official who was supposedly "following up" on the cheque on my behalf, I overheard him wryly ask another:

"Why are we giving Baccus Matthews' daughter this money

anyway?"

"She aced the national exam," his colleague replied, "the Government has a policy of arranging sponsorship for the dux."

"I think we should reserve such opportunities for people who really need it, not her. Her father has money and can afford to send his daughter to any school in the world," he spat out angrily.

And so, just like that, moments later, I was told the cheque had gone missing.

I was being denied a scholarship opportunity by a Liberian official simply because I was a Matthews. How could something I worked for, qualified for, and clearly earned by merit, become political? What did my father's politics have to do with my exam results? Should a deserving candidate be denied a merit-based opportunity simply because of who his/her parents are? I recall how hard I had studied after moving home from Abidjan, the number of recreational activities and visits to cousins I had declined to effectively transition from the Ivorian French-speaking school system back to Liberia's English curriculum. So, for the life of me, I could not understand why an opportunity that would be granted to any other deserving Liberian would not materialize in my case, simply because I was "Baccus Matthews' daughter." As I was learning, this, too, is what it meant to be a Matthews.

A short while after that, I discovered that the Government of Morocco had offered Liberia several scholarships as part of its bilateral scholarship program. The documents had all arrived in Arabic and French, the official languages of the Kingdom. I immediately offered my services to translate the documents from French to English at no charge to the

Ministry of Education. Still pursuing avenues to further my education, I looked forward to the opportunity to do so in Rabat. There was an aptitude test administered, I passed with flying colors. There were documents required, all of which I carefully submitted, but when the list came out of those shortlisted, strangely enough, once again, I did not make the cut.

One ministry official advised that my Dad and I consider "encouraging" the process to get my name on the final list—he was requesting a bribe. Appalled at his move to compromise my nascent integrity, I had had enough. I walked away from any further discussions and set my eyes on the renowned Biological Science Program at the University of Ghana instead, working towards the next possible intake. Pending admission, I decided I would work in the meantime, and so, with guidance from one of my amazing Aunts, I landed my first real job at the tender age of 17.

***

When you grow up in a home with a protective father, ever watchful brothers, and so many other male figures keeping watch over you and making sure you are safe, it is easy to believe that every man is a protector. It is relatively easy to think that every man is a friend and not a foe and that every boy you meet is as sweet, well-intentioned, and well-mannered as your brothers. After all, that is what you know.

When I was 13, Dad once got upset about me sitting on a male cousin's lap. I saw nothing of it, of course. We were all playing video games, the living room was crowded, all the other seats were taken, so naturally, I sat on a cousin's lap. Dad was furious! He took me aside and sternly warned:

"I don't want you sitting on any man's lap, you hear? No

cousin, no brother, no friend. No male laps, period."

"Yes, Dad," I replied, eyes downcast and shoulders bowed. My innocent mind could not fathom the harm that would lead to.

He tried to warn me about the dynamics of the male-female relationship and the need for caution, but did not want me sailing through life bridled by fear of the opposite sex. After tales of Cinderella, Snow White, Romeo, and Juliet, he needed me to learn that there was more to a relationship between a woman and a man, a girl, and a boy than fairytales and happy endings. But how do you explain that to your 13-year-old without leaving her jaded?

He gave me a book to read: Nathaniel Hawthorne's *The Scarlet Letter,* a story centered on the power of a woman's silence. By giving me a book, he knew I would read, he attempted to subtly pass a message I needed to hear.

The Scarlet Letter tells the story of Hester Prynne, a young married woman who got into an adulterous affair and wound up pregnant in the Puritan society of New England. Hawthorne takes you straight to the scene of her trial for adultery, where she is placed on a pedestal of shame in the market square for all to see. The crowd hurls and hoots at her, calling her many defaming names. Before the eyes of all, under the scorching sun, with her precious baby girl nestled in her arms, Hester is repeatedly asked to name her fellow adulterer and give her child a father—thereby lessening her sentence. But Hester sits there silent.

She knows she would be a pariah for the rest of her life. Hester knows she'd have to spend the rest of her days ostracized from society and her nights banished from human interaction. She knows she would be sentenced to wearing a bold scarlet "A" for adultery emblazoned over her heart for the rest of her life, but for all the punishment in the world, Hester would not name the father of her child. To the point where the Minister leading the hearing of the case blurts out:

"Wondrous strength and generosity of a woman's heart, she will not speak[53]."

It was Robert Louis Stevenson that said: *"The cruelest lies are often told in silence[54]."* After several hours and attempts, Hester, resolute, says nothing. She is sentenced to a life of seclusion, living outside the Puritan settlement. She is made an example of, so others would never dare follow suit in sinful trespass; thus, becoming the embodiment of the scarlet letter.

Hawthorne goes on to narrate how Hester so courageously rose above her circumstances, making a name and livelihood through her superior dressmaking skills while enduring emotional torment from her aged husband, Roger Chillingworth. He just so happened to arrive from England the day Hester was made to sit in shame in the market square. The story concludes by unveiling Hester's partner in sin. None other than the good Reverend Arthur Dimmesdale, the very Minister leading her questioning during the trial! Unbelievable, right?

By urging me to read Hester's story, my father shrewdly tried to teach me that people are never what they seem, and sometimes the people you least expect are the most duplicitous of us all. He was showing me the depth of a woman's silence. Hester raised her child as a single mother when singlehood was considered a pariah in a highly conservative society and endured everything—the stigma, the shame, the sentence, and never uttered a word.

While I appreciated the book as a remarkable piece of literature, my teenage reasoning was limited in fully connecting the warning more personally in my interactions with the opposite sex. Later, I would find out that my innocent trust in the male gender, based on the sheltered, loving environment I was raised in, had nothing to do with all men and what some are truly capable of. A lesson I would painfully learn the hard way just 4 years later.

***

His family had known mine for many years, so he was quite welcomed around the house. My perspective, skewed by the haven my brothers always seemed to provide, never once suspected any ill intent. Then it happened.

He reached out in what seemed to be a kiss, but before I could realize it, he thrust one firm grasp around my throat, pinning me down; with the other, he covered my mouth. His pants fell to the floor. I fought, but he was stronger. I cried for help, but with his hand sealing my mouth shut, my screams were muffled. I struggled to roll over, to break free, but clearly, he was better prepared for the tussle than I was. When fighting back seemed futile, I did the only thing else I could do, I shut my eyes, blocked out the scene as he violently crushed his body against mine.

Moments later, he was done. It all ended as forcefully and as brutally as it began. Try as I may; it is a scene that stays with me for life. Time stood still. Even longer than the 36 hours I spent laboriously bringing my first child into the world was that half-hour ordeal that day. In his abrasive grip, I went from being a self-assured, budding teenage girl, full of bright hopes and dreams, to shattered glass.

My innocence, so safely guarded through the tricky teenage years of prom dates and peer pressure, was viciously snatched—robbed at the hands of someone I knew and trusted. Lying there in utter disbelief, I shivered as the foul mixture of blood and semen found its way down my thighs. For a moment, I blackout, totally unaware of my surroundings. I knew of rape; I had narrowly escaped it at the hands of rebels just a year before. I had heard about it happening to others but never had I ever thought it would happen to me—especially at the hands of someone so close.

Till my dying day, I will never forget the look on his face as he got up, wiping the sweat off his face, pulling up his pants, with a smug glimmer in his eyes, jubilant at his conquest. I lay there in complete shock. Shame. Horror. Regret. I could no longer scream. I could barely move. In the stench of the moment, agonizing tears streamed down my cheeks. The assault may have lasted just about half an hour, but that was enough. Thirty minutes was all it took to dim the sparkle in my eye and quench the fire in my soul. A part of me died that day, killed by someone I least expected— someone I thought was practically family.

***

We have all broken porcelain at some point in our lives; a plate, a bowl, Dad's favorite mug, Grandma's hand-painted flower vase. At some point or another, delicate things have accidentally slipped out of our hands and onto the hardwood floors, crashing into several mendable pieces. We have often been able to whisk out a magical adhesive and purposefully glue the broken pieces back together nearly as neatly and elegantly as they once were.

The same cannot be said of broken glass. In terms of chemical composition, glass and porcelain are manufactured from quite different raw materials. Glass is made by melting sand with a mixture of soda, potash, and lime. Glass tends to be more fragile. Throw glass to the floor, and that is the end of it. It would break into so many pieces with countless scattered splinters that you realize you are better off replacing rather than ever mending shattered glass. When you rape someone, you break their pristine soul, crush their spirit, leaving them nearly impossible to fix.

That dreadful night, I became shattered glass, the splinters of my once indomitable spirit scattered despairingly across the floor. On the surface, I was still Magdalene Matthews. My parents' only daughter. My brothers' only sister. Neither name nor physique had changed, but my spirit was now crushed with the most tragic blow a person could ever endure. I was deprived of my right to choose. Forced into a state of silence.

I had grown up loved, protected, sheltered, carefully watched over by the many men in my life. Yet, the day it would matter the most, there was no one around.

Then as if the wounds already inflicted were not enough, he added something more lethal; the dagger of words: *"You are nothing! You have been made to believe you were extra your whole life, but you are nothing!"*

Still catching his breath, he made sure to say it one more time, ensuring it registered into my broken, bleeding soul: *"You don't compare in any way to the girls I have been with. Do you hear me? You are nothing!"*

My flowing tears were my only reply.

"YOU ARE NOTHING" became three words that would cling to me like a cloak for years. Three words that would replay in my spirit ever so loudly each time I failed a test. Each time, I was not selected for a job. Each time, I was turned down for a scholarship. Author Lorraine Nilon calls it *"soul abuse,"* that is, *"the destruction of a victim's awareness of the strength within their soul,"* stemming *"from the* *abuser's intention to corrupt another's understanding of their own significance[55]."*

For years, those words would form the lenses through which I filtered life's disappointments. It would take intentional self-affirmation, uplifting books, counseling, prayers, and positivity to rebuild my self-esteem and undo the damage caused that day. This is the first time I am publicly narrating this in such detail. Many friends and relations reading this will be learning of this here for the very first time. Please accept my sincere apologies for the myriad of emotions this may arouse. My journey to closure required owning my truth, acknowledging deep-seated pain while depriving my silence of the yoke it so tauntingly held over my life for nearly two decades.

By now, some of you may be asking: "Maggie, why didn't you say something?"

Countless times over the years, I, too, have asked myself, "Maggie, why didn't you come forward? Report the incident to your parents? Or tell your friends? Why not, even your siblings?"

Like Hester Prynne, for years, I wore my scarlet badge of shame in silence. I did not come forward because I knew all too well how the story would end. My Dad was far too known, and my last name was far too recognized to have come out, then and there. The 17-year-old me could not have borne the burden of the prying eyes, the media coverage, and the judgment from the court of public opinion that would have ensued. It also just did not seem like something you shared on the phone or ruined a memorable family vacation recounting. So, I kept quiet.

Nobel Laureate and activist Leymah Gbowee would weigh in on this in the Liberian context in a recent social media post entitled *Warrior Princesses:*

> *"It is no secret that Liberia has a terrible and destructive "don't ask don't tell culture" when it comes to rape and the abuse of women and girls. We have normalized sweeping the subject of sexual violence under the rug because it makes families and communities look bad. So, when a person finally breaks the silence and speaks out, they, in turn, look like the abnormal one[56]."*

Just months before, Liberia had come to know me as the only girl out of four students nationwide to ace the WAEC exams with flying colors. I was in no way equipped mentally or emotionally to handle the public criticism, pointed fingers, and invasion of privacy that would have accompanied the courageous sharing of my truth. That doesn't mean I didn't try, though.

The first person I ever felt comfortable enough to vulnerably share that nightmare with told me it was my fault—as if there ever is a justifiable reason to violate another. Sadly, I believed him at the time; and so, I quickly kept quiet. He was my litmus test for whether I was ready to face the court of public opinion. I clearly was not. I chose the armor of silence to protect me from the stigma I knew would come should anyone hear of that tragic night. I allowed the ordeal to seep into my subconscious, away from the light of day. I did my best to put the "past" behind me. Yet when abuse is left unaddressed, it never is truly "past."

Dear reader, if you have suffered some form of abuse or the other in your lifetime—sexual, emotional, or physical, I need you to know it was **NOT** your fault. It does not matter what you were wearing, where you were, and who you were with. No one—ABSOLUTELY NO ONE had the right to deprive you of your right to choose. A person's choice, a person's will, is such a powerful thing. The entire premise of modern religion is hinged on the principle of a person's right to choose—free will. The whole strength of democracy is predicated on the platform of a person's right to choose his/her preferred candidate. When that right is taken from you, it is an assassination of the soul, an afront on the very nature of who we are as humans. It is a violation of the fundamentals of our shared humanity.

Likewise, if you or someone you know tends to minimize a person's experience of abuse, please stop. By discounting survivors, you invalidate a person's lived experience and make it harder for people to speak up and chart their path towards inner healing.

***

With everything life had thrown at me, I walked out of my teens and into my twenties as a very bruised and broken person. The years 2003 and 2004 proved to be pivotal turning points in my life. I endured some of my most significant tests and trials. Not only did I have to craft an escape plan out of a country in conflict all by myself at the tender age of 16 and stay sane enough to pull it off, but at 17, I also experienced the deepest, most unspoken shattering of my soul.

By the time I turned 20, I had seen way too many things I could never unsee, had been to places I wish I had never been, and had experienced things I could never forget.

Despite everything happening in and around me, something deep within the inner recesses of my soul chose a greater destiny—a future far better than the hands of cards I was dealt.

So, I kept pressing on, undeterred, in the words of William Ernest Henley,

"My head was bloody but UNBOWED[57]."

115

IT'S A SHE

***

116

Chapter 6

Legon Days

"If you run into the woman I am meant to be, tell her that I'm doing everything I can today to meet her tomorrow[58]."

Sarah Jakes Roberts, Author, and Renowned Speaker

The University of Ghana (UG), Legon campus, will always represent hallowed grounds for me because behind those white-washed walls, I morphed from an uncertain, questioning 18-year-old to a fighting young woman. Surrounded by 7 square miles of colonial-style architecture and characteristic clay roofs, Legon is where I got my wings and first learned to use them.

There were many of life's lessons learned in the halls of the Zoology Department, and tears shed in the labs of the Chemistry Building. How could I ever forget the study all-nighters and the buzzing mosquitoes in the windy, cold corridors of the Statistics Department? How about the dusk-to-dawn assignment-typing marathons in the Legon Dining Hall and the early morning exams written at the infamous Great Hall? I reflect with a smile, overwhelmed by pure nostalgia. Ah! Those were the priceless ingredients in making notable men and women, true to UG's motto, *"Integri Procedamus,"* meaning in the pursuit of integrity. No doubt, greatness emerges in obscurity, genius is birthed in the dark, and masterpieces are created in the shadows.

***

By January 2005, Liberia was now finally at peace with herself. The Accra Comprehensive Peace Agreement had been signed two years before, giving the nation a fresh lease on life after a decade and a half of conflict. Thousands of peacekeepers had been deployed to keep the peace, support the National Transitional Government of Liberia, headed by Chairman Charles Gyude Bryant, and pave the way for General and Presidential elections in October. It was the most exciting time, politically and economically, in the country's recent history. Liberia was back!

Everything, it seemed, was happening all at once. The entire country needed to be rebuilt from the ground up, and it was going to take millions in investments and all hands-on deck. Former combatants and child soldiers were being disarmed, demobilized, and reintegrated into active social life. UN operations across the peacekeeping mission, agencies, funds, and programs continued to expand daily to cover the country's entire length and breadth. Liberia had come alive, and so had we, her people.

The level of optimism across the nation was infectious. As repatriation exercises were underway, people returned to Liberia in droves from neighboring countries, resettling and rebuilding their lives in the place they called home. Structures were going up every single day. People were rebuilding houses, entrepreneurs were starting businesses, and the broader business community was massively investing in real estate to accommodate what would be the single largest UN presence in any one nation at the time. All eyes were on Liberia, and there was a demonstrated commitment to help the country finally turn the page on the era of war.

In this massive wave of dynamism and anticipation, I transitioned from the local commercial bank where I had landed my first job to start working with a UN agency in Voinjama City, the scenic capital of Lofa County in the northern tip of Liberia. I was still awaiting my University of Ghana admission letter, so I strategically continued enhancing my resume until then.

Once known as the "breadbasket of the nation" before the war, Lofa County was now the epicenter of nation-building. It was a major hub for refugee repatriation and reintegration. Yet, it was still considered rebel-held territory, being the LURD rebel group's stronghold.

The joy on the faces of people returning home, reuniting with their families after escaping months before with nothing more than their babies strapped to their backs, is something I will never forget. The fulfillment that came with being at the forefront of refugee repatriation from neighboring Guinea and Sierra Leone gave me such a thrill I cannot quite explain. For the first time in years of conflict, there was so much international commitment towards lasting peace that we could not help but contribute as Liberians.

I was hired to do mainly office work, but how could I resist being out in the field in the thick of the nation-rebuilding? Given the workload, it had to be all hands-on deck. So, I quickly cleared up my office tasks in the morning hours and dashed into the field to help in every way I could. There too, my French linguistic skills came in handy many times to communicate with the returnees from neighboring Guinea, especially the small children, who, like sponges, had so quickly absorbed the language spoken in their country of refuge.

Coming into development work from the banking sector, Voinjama was where I traded in my dark corporate suits and 4-inch heels for rugged jeans, UN-branded t-shirts, and sneakers. I did everything from helping to hold babies, communicating in French with the children, assessing latrines, and transporting items around the center. Water and sanitation, as a profession, had not yet crept their way into my heart. Still, I remember being particularly interested in the WASH facilities and the protection issues discussed during meetings surrounding the safety of women and children accessing the latrines at night.

Given my Dad's political involvement, taking up an assignment in "rebel territory," still undergoing disarmament, was a really daring thing to do. The move was not without risks to my personal safety. Yet, the thought of being a part of something so monumental in Liberia's history so inspired me that I was willing to take on the risk. I was being allowed to be a part of something far greater than myself, something so meaningful in my nation's recovery, I had to help drive the process. With much of my childhood plagued by war, this was the chance to rebuild, and I was ready to contribute.

Back then, the living conditions in Lofa were nothing compared to Monrovia. Just getting there, given the deplorable road conditions, was a feat on its own. The drive from Monrovia down south along the Atlantic coast to mountainous Voinjama up north could take anywhere between 9-12 hours. Meanwhile, that half-day drive was only possible thanks to recent road works by the

UN peacekeepers' engineering battalion. There was no running water, no electricity, no cell phone coverage, and no sanitation conditions in most parts of the city. Houses up for rent had been destroyed by shelling and required massive renovation to get a single room fit-for-purpose. You would be fortunate to find a place to stay that had a functioning latrine.

On top of that, everything had to be brought from Monrovia—everything from milk to toiletries. Shops carried products brought in from neighboring Guinea, but these were sold at high prices. Thus, a renovation was quite an investment, but that was just a small part of the sacrifices to be made if one was to live and work in Voinjama at the time.

I managed to find a vacant room in a house of 5 bedrooms that needed serious repair. The landlord, who occupied the bedroom furthest down the hall, was renting out the remaining 4. He had gotten tenants for 3, mine being the only vacant room left. It would cost me several hundred dollars to get the roof fixed, door adequately locked, and windows burglar-proofed enough to occupy it safely. The shared, outside bathroom was a mat and twig installation that offered very little privacy. I would have to wake up in the blistering morning cold to bathe while still dark in the shoddy structure. There was no toilet. I had to rush across town to the office on a motorbike each time I needed to use the bathroom, even on weekends and late at night. At least there, I was sure of a functioning toilet.

With promising NGO activity taking place in the country, my older cousin, Adolphus, followed me to Lofa in the hopes of finding work himself while keeping an eye on me in the LURD stronghold. Despite the relocation and living challenges and the apparent security concerns, none of that seemed to bother me.

In Lofa, I discovered pristine Liberia, and I loved it. The greenery of the hills, the freshness of the air, the people's relaxed nature, and the simplicity of life enthralled me. People did not have much, but they were so happy. Friday market days brought the city to life, with tens of marketeers coming in from neighboring towns and villages to sell fresh produce and trade goods. The peppers sold were so fresh, the snails so huge, and the ambiance so warm.

Motorbike, or "pem-pem," as we called it, was the primary means of transport around Voinjama. On weekends, I would ride up the many hills scattered across the city, just to overlook life happening down below. During the memorable months in Lofa, I had my very first taste of porcupine gravy and other types of bushmeat. I ate "torborgee," the famous Lofa delicacy prepared by the local women, using the right mix of traditional oil and ingredients. I met people who looked forward to each sunrise and were grateful for each peaceful sunset now that the war was finally over. A sight to behold was when the children would come out to play football on the open field at the Voinjama Multilateral High School. The bliss of childhood, liberated from the shackles of war, beamed across their tiny faces. How I admired their resilience! Little by little, with remarkable determination, the Lofians would repair portions of their homes destroyed during the shelling. There, on the green hills of Voinjama, I discovered a Liberia that would capture my heart and forever hold it captive.

I owe a lot to Liberia, Africa's oldest Republic. Liberia gave me a cultural identity and a rich heritage, which I will always treasure. I would later leave Lofa and its charms to head off to college once my admission confirmation arrived from the University of Ghana. Life and work have taken me to many other parts of Liberia since then. I have explored the rich, historical heritage of Cape Palmas, the serenity of

Sanniquellie, and the delectable seafood of Robertsport. Still, something about the soothing freshness of the air that kisses my cheeks each time I stand on the serene Lofa hills is a memory that stays with me. Personally, and professionally, my 2005 assignment in Voinjama City evokes such fond memories I will forever cherish.

***

When I first landed at the University of Ghana's campus in September 2005, I was a vastly different person from who I was finishing high school two years before. I had evolved, somehow mutated into another version of myself. I went from being this poised, bright-eyed teenager, full of hope and promise, into this insecure, marred young woman. I had become a shattered-glass version of myself.

I carried the weight of a secret that I had told no one. I had not allowed myself time to fully process and come to terms with what had happened to me that fateful night in 2004. I numbed my emotions and tried to move on. I allowed myself to think that it was all just a bad dream, a nightmare that would somehow go away. As a coping mechanism, I allowed myself to live in denial, refusing to accept the truth of the horrific ordeal that would only come to haunt me in the years ahead. I had not healed, and I certainly wasn't whole. Yet, the days came and went, so I just continued living. I decided to throw myself into the competitive rat race of academic life.

My first year was rough. I had been out of school for over two years, so I clearly needed time to readjust to intense academic work. All forms of quadratic equations had evaporated from my brain. My classmates, mostly coming in fresh from 4 years of boarding school in different parts of Ghana, settled relatively smoothly into the communal

123

college dorm life. I, on the other hand, had several tasks at hand. First, I had to settle into a new country, acclimatize to its scorching heat and sweaty humidity, and learn to enjoy completely different food from the rice and sauce staple I was used to in Liberia. I also had to make new friends and catch a few Twi words[v] to help me get around while keeping up impressive grades. It was a lot to adjust to.

By my second year, Level 200, things started to fall in line. My roommate, Awo, had adopted me as her Liberian sister, giving me a family environment with delicious home-cooked meals away from home. Her mom, Mommy Rosie, would always save me a hearty bowl of fufu and light soup on weekends. The little Twi I managed to learn was never enough for lengthy chats with Mommy Rosie, who insisted on chatting with me only in the local language. Still, we would laughingly converse anyway.

That year, two exciting things happened. First, I got to accompany Dad to Ma Ellen's inauguration in January, and secondly in the summer, I stumbled on my career calling. After visiting my folks in Liberia over Christmas, I flew back to Liberia during the summer break from school to assume a short work contract to earn some extra cash for my upkeep in Legon. In Monrovia, I found my professional purpose.

During a visit to one of the slum communities, I would have the epiphany that would redirect my career path, thrusting me into the open arms of the environmental health field of water, sanitation, and hygiene. My "water romance," as I call it, would ignite in the vibrant streets of New Kru Town.

It was one of those days that Dad had decided to visit long-time friends and partisans in New Kru Town, on Bushrod Island. Nestled on the corner of the Atlantic Ocean and the Saint Paul River estuary, New Kru Town is known for

v Ghana's most widely spoken vernacular

its high population density and fisher-folk inhabitants. As Dad and UPP party sympathizers engaged in their usual political discussions, I took the liberty to walk around the block, familiarizing myself with the popular Redemption Hospital community.

As I strolled slowly through the close-quartered homes and bustling street corners, I noticed a young woman sitting by an open fire, preparing cornmeal for her infant son. He crawled happily in the dirt nearby—enjoying the simple joy of childhood. I stood there for a while, taking in the adorable scene. I watched her lovingly cook, take her time to feed her baby the warm yellow cereal, and then give him water to drink out of a small blue cup. The magic of the moment quickly faded away as I noted in disbelief the level of muddy residue lurking snuggly at the bottom of the transparent plastic bucket, she had stored her household drinking water in.

"How could they possibly drink and cook with such unsafe water," I wondered? It is an image I could not shake.

I found myself genuinely concerned about the child's well-being. What happens if he falls ill? I felt intensely triggered to act and help secure safe water access for this family. How could society spare him the burden of disease and his parents, the cost of care? How could I help?

The heavens opened into a light drizzle as the sun remained high in the afternoon sky. I knew then and there I had found my career calling. I was 19 years old, in the slums of Monrovia, when I fell in love with safe water, and it is a love I have held onto ever since.

When I later told my Dad, I would be trading in every parent's dream—med-school plans for public health, focusing on water, sanitation, and hygiene (WASH), he knew I had not made the decision on a whim. So passionate was I for WASH that 2 years ahead of my undergraduate dissertation, I had already developed an extensive water testing research proposal that I began shopping around to local donors and non-governmental organizations (NGOs) in the hopes of securing funding. Kindred spirits, Dad knew I meant business.

Since then, safe water for all is a fundamental human right that I have dedicated my career to helping realize. Some of my fondest work-related memories are of water testing trips across Liberia. I would travel to the field to collect samples and test water from various hand-pumps and water points in Cape Mount, Lofa, and Nimba counties. With Liberia's post-war road conditions, the arduous drive to these locations could take several hours by road. But once there, an overwhelming enthusiasm would kick in; my nerdy juices would come alive. I would don my crispy-starched white lab coat, engineering boots and dash out to do what I love.

At the various community hand-pumps, the children would rush out and form a circle around my workspace, curious to see what I was up to. I would brief the community residents on the purpose of my stop, telling them in simple Liberian English that I was there to "look inside their water" and see if it was safe to drink. Their excitement was so palpable. Some would bring benches out to sit and watch me work. In a place where most technicians and engineers who showed up to discuss water issues with the community were male, I was a welcomed anomaly. I was young, female, and with my sophisticated testing equipment, I was doing something they clearly had not seen before. I was not there to dig a new well, erect a new pump, or market a water treatment product like filters, chlorine tablets, or hypochlorite solutions. I was there to tell them if their drinking water was safe, and I would perform the chemical and bacteriological tests right in front of them to prove it. They naturally appreciated the gesture.

To the adults, my presence there was the chemistry class they never got growing up. For the kids, it was an orientation into career pathways. Either way, to these people, I was a thing of national pride. I would open my test kit, and piece by piece, the kids would ask what each instrument was, what it was used for and how this calculator-like instrument could tell if the water was safe or not. The girls were incredibly excited to see another girl doing something so complex. I would let them ask as many questions as possible, stretching the limits of their imagination. After running the various tests and collecting much-needed data, I would always seize the opportunity to encourage the kids to study hard and consider going into the sciences.

In the 21st century, STEM (Science, Technology, Engineering, and Maths) education is crucial to nation-building. I always urge students, especially in the developing world, to consider it a career path whenever I have the chance. I will never be able to change everything in the world. Still, if I can make sure children in Africa have clean water to drink each day, I would have done something, in some way, in my own little corner, to help make the world a better place.

***

By the time I walked out of the walls of Ghana's premier university in 2009, practically every Professor who had ever taught me knew me by name and nationality. So much life happened in those four incredible years that, at one point or another, I had to show up at their offices, engage in coursework, or submit assignments on behalf of my classmates as Class Representative.

Another area I stood out in was when it came to the questions I asked and answered in class. There seems to be an unspoken rule in Ghana that students do not ask questions during a lecture. They only respond to questions individually directed at them and do so to signal who the "sharks," or the brains, in the pack are. They say little else otherwise. I, on the contrary, asked many questions and responded even when I wasn't sure of the answer. With so few of us participating in class, it didn't take long for my glasses-rimmed face and foreign accent to standout. How could I just sit there?

For us, foreign students at the University of Ghana, the prospect of sitting on the same bench and being taught by the same Professors cost thousands of dollars more as compared to our Ghanaian counterparts. My husband, Dennis, and I were classmates, taking practically the same classes, yet his tuition was but a tiny fraction of mine. With what it cost me each semester and the hurdles I was jumping through to stay in school, how could I afford to merely spectate? I entered each lecture with my A-game, ready to maximize the moment and learn as much as possible. Where some students saw Legon as their first wild taste of freedom from the proverbial nest of conservative upbringing and strict boarding schools, I saw it as an expensive piece to a puzzle that I could not afford to lose sight of.

As they say: *"School days are the best days;"* my journey through the University of Ghana-Legon was indeed an amazing one. When it came to room and board, I was quite adventurous. In four years, I went from lodging at the off-campus Ages Abba Hostel in my first year, to Pentagon Hostels in my third, and lastly, the International Students' Hostel (ISH) in my senior year. It was in the halls of ISH that I, along with visiting students from Tufts and other US exchange universities, huddled around the TV in the hostel's Common Room in 2008 to watch Barack Obama's history-making acceptance speech as 44th President of the United States. With each new room came new roommates, I established valuable friendships that I maintain to this day.

My favorite place on campus was the Balme Library. I would spend many days and nights in its quiet corridors, studying, reading, and researching. With its notable colonial architecture, the Balme Library, named after the University's first Principal, sits in the heart of the campus, a stone-throw from the Faculty of Science[59]. My Legon days were very memorable moments. I met world-class professors and matured considerably, away from the familiarity of home. I learned the value of being open to different experiences, cultures, and cuisines, values that would come in handy many years later in married life. For all the nostalgia they bring, my college days were not without their share of challenges.

***

It was Friday, August 22, 2008. I remember the date well because it was the last day for registration for the 2008-2009 academic year. If you attended UG back then, you would recall just how tedious the registration process was. It was an endless line-up of queues. Queues at the bank to pay your fees. Queues at the Great Hall to enlist on the University's database. Queues to register with the Students Representative Council. Queues to check in with your assigned hall or Junior Common Room. Queues at the Faculty of Science. Queues at every department, and for foreign students, additional queues at the International Programs Office.

The current generation can be grateful to the IT gurus that

a lot more is being done online. Back then, registration was the least sensational back-to-school task. Yet, once classes began, you were immersed into an unparalleled learning experience covering your chosen major, computer literacy, statistics, and African studies, producing versatile graduates, forward-looking into the future yet deeply rooted in their rich ancestry.

School had reopened a few weeks before, and the campus had come alive to the hustle and bustle of students moving in. For incoming freshmen, their parents tagged along in overstuffed cars transporting fridges, microwaves, and rice cookers. They were embarking on their first year, fresh as can be, eager and expectant. This would be their proverbial first taste of freedom from the rigors of boarding schools and the watchful eyes at home. The college move represented a rite of passage into adulthood, which they couldn't wait to embark on.

For me, this was senior year, and it sure was not starting as bright and beautiful as it was for most of these starry-eyed freshmen. Despite the numerous challenges I had faced up to that point, somehow, I had miraculously managed to get through three years in Legon. I have to admit, it was a blockbuster-worthy marathon struggle. I had gone from "struggling to start" to "struggling to leave," then "struggling to stay," to "struggling to cope"—all while maintaining good grades. I was on the 4th and final lap— "struggling to finish."

By the time the calendar flipped into August 2008, I owed the University of Ghana $9,898.98. Arrears from the year before when Dad was sick had added to this year's fees, yielding a grand total of a notable series of nines and eights. Numerologists would have had a field day.

That summer, I had dedicated all my time writing letters to companies that I thought could help sponsor my tuition. I used my convincing 3rd year straight A's transcript as my selling point. By July, I had dropped off letters at nearly every major bank, mining, beverage, and food-processing company in Accra. One after the other, the company managers would phone me with apologies. The more companies declined, the more other companies I approached. I look back at those days with a smile because, despite the disappointments, I developed valuable fundraising and corporate engagement skills in return. I was quite strategic in my approach. I had a list of 30 companies of various sizes scattered across the city. I made sure to hand-deliver each letter with an attached copy of my transcript and water testing research proposal to prove my potential. My buddy Patience Saaka and I jokingly called it "intellectual begging." After all, what did I have to lose? I had accumulated 9,898 reasons to keep trying. I had come too far to give up.

The University Counselor, Mr. Croffet, one of the most remarkable people I have ever met, was also on the lookout for sponsorships for me. He reached out to people within his network, scouting for support, irrespective of the amount. It would have been more convenient for Mr. Croffet to raise funds for Ghanaian students in need. Their fees were considerably less than mine, a foreign student, but somehow, Mr. Croffet took an interest in my case and was determined to see to it that I finished.

My college years taught me the value of being open and receptive to help from people whose only connection to you is the unflinching belief in your success. Legon helped me rebuild the trust I had lost many years before when my own government gave me the walk-around on an opportunity, I so rightfully deserved. Here my grades, not my last name or my father's politics, did the talking. You can argue with many things, but as they say, *"you cannot argue with results."* The grades on my transcript echoed my results.

Life has a way of making skeptics out of us, suspicious of the authenticity of another's actions. My Legon days taught me: 1) the simplicity of giving life my best shot, and 2) there still are well-meaning people in the world whose sole motive is to help you progress.

The initial weeks for registration had come and gone; school authorities extended the deadline by a few more days at a late fee, and I still had not registered. My faith went from fervent hot, and hopeful to dry and desperate as classes commenced. August 22, 2008, was the final deadline. If I hadn't registered by then, I would have to defer the academic year. Considering everything I had gotten through to that point, I had to give it a final push.

***

The day before, I had locked myself in my room the entire day, praying, thinking, and strategizing on my next course of action. I went through my phonebook once more, searching for who I could reach out to, given the short timeline. I phoned several contacts, including very close friends of my late Dad; none could come through at the time. In a final push of faith, I decided to dash to the Great Hall, the University of Ghana's administration block, to talk the Business Manager into helping buy me a bit more time.

That was when it happened.

The trigger, the initial push, call it the very first spark that would inspire me to someday write this book and share my story in all its collateral beauty.

I got to the Great Hall at nearly 2pm. The administrators

had all gone to a meeting. Other students turned to leave; I did not have that luxury. I decided to sit and wait.

Nearly two hours later, the University's Business Manager returned. His secretary advised that I wait. Again, I had nowhere else to go, so I waited. It was past 4pm, all the banks were now closed. It was clear that my window of opportunity was getting slimmer by the minute. Going through another mental exercise of alternate solutions, I look up and recognize the accountant, with his car keys in hand, heading for the parking lot through another door. He was leaving without meeting me!

I chase him down the hall, introducing myself and pitching my case as quickly as I could while running down the concrete stairs. I told him I had recently lost my Dad and was having a few financial challenges but would cover the outstanding fees over time, provided he gave me a chance. I point to the 3.79 GPA boldly sprawled across the top of my transcript, proof that despite everything, I still delivered.

We approach his parked brown BMW. He paused, and for the first time, took a long, scrutinizing look at me. It was as if he was administering a visual polygraph to assess the veracity of my story. Then with creased brows, he let his thoughts flood out:

"Young lady, this is a university, the premier university of the Republic of Ghana. This is not a charity institution. Now, I have heard your sob story, but there are countless sob stories out there, my dear. How is yours any different?"

He looked around, seeking approbation from bystanders, who were all now entirely fixated on us. Between the staffers on their way home, students concluding registration, and those buying late afternoon drinks at the nearby snack post, there were now at least 25 pairs of eyes staring at me.

I fought back the hot tears welling up in mine. My tongue stuck helplessly to my palate.

"Young lady, listen, I know I cannot afford Oxford and Cambridge, so I dare not send my kids there. If you cannot afford the small fees we charge foreign students here, why bother coming? Why come to Legon if you know you cannot afford it? You are merely occupying the space that could have been given to another deserving Ghanaian student."

His words stung, but he was not quite finished. He opened the door to his brown BMW, eased his way into the driver's seat, and popped on his AC.

"You are expected to pay 70% of your fees and register here at the Great Hall by 5pm tomorrow. Failure to do so, I suggest you come back next year or just go where you can afford. Look, my dear, like I said, we are not running a charity institution here."

Slamming his door shut, he drove away, leaving my stunned body at the mercy of the onlookers. I had never been so publicly humiliated my entire life. I understand he was doing his job. Of course, as UG Accountant, he had to make sure the books were balanced, the lights were on, and the staff paid, but to so reduce me in the process?

On that August afternoon, thanks to him, I made a solemn promise to myself. I vowed that I would succeed, come what may and that my story, this story, would be written and serve as a hug to someone who would need it as desperately as I did that day. On August 21, 2008, I promised myself that I would make it in this life; as TD Jakes says, "Come hell or high water." I would own my narrative, and someday, I would share the story of my Legon experience and ensure his contribution was chronicled. Maya Angelou once said:

"You may encounter many defeats, but you must not be defeated. In fact, it may be necessary to encounter the defeats, so you can know who you are, what you can rise from, how you can still come out of it[60]."

Whenever I reflect on that August, I remember that day as one of the defining moments that pushed me. I have Mr. Brown BMW, the accountant to thank for helping me discover the depth of ashes I was ready to rise from.

Slowly but surely, I walked down the Lower Hill, leading away from the Great Hall, not with a payment plan as I had initially hoped but with a kindled zeal to find a way out. I was determined to complete my final year, and his condescension would not stop me. I did the math; 70% of $9898.98 was a little over $6,000. Mr. Croffet and I had managed to raise $3,000. All I needed was another $3,000 to get my name on the list. In his classic piece, *Harlem,* poet Langston Hughes asks a compelling question: *"What happens to a dream deferred?"* He then surmises:

"Does it dry up like a raisin in the sun?
Or fester like a sore- And then run?
Does it stink like rotten meat?
Or crust and sugar over- like a syrupy sweet?
Maybe it just sags like a heavy load.
Or does it explode [61]?"

I asked myself what would happen if my dream was deferred. I could hardly bear the thought. I had come too far, sacrificed so much, studied my way through three years of uncertainty and the loss of my Dad just a year before; how could I possibly defer the dream now that I had only one year left? I decided to take one last scroll through my phonebook and let God handle the rest.

Suddenly, it hit me.

There was still one person I had not called. I hurriedly dial. The phone rings several times. Considering the time difference, "they must be sleeping," I say to myself. I slowly hang up. Crushed, I reach for the light switch over my bed, but just as I turn off the lights, my phone rings. "Hello?"

I cut to the chase. I blurt out everything in less than 30 seconds and pause to hear the response. She listens and promises to get back to me. Hope is reborn. I decide I can hold on to that for a few more hours. I can hold on to hope. I say one final heartfelt prayer and head to bed.

The next morning, I wake up to a call. It is my mother. As promised, the family pulled through, and the funds would be sent to me that very day. I shower and dress up, compile all my documents needed for registration, and scurry out to the Ecobank branch on campus.

The tiny banking hall was full that day. Students and parents lined up to deposit school and hostel fees on the final day of registration. I take a seat in the corner. The line moves, customers come and go, but my attention is fixed on my phone.

"Hey Magdalene, how are you? Great to see you! I can see you had a good break!"

It is Dela, a fellow classmate majoring in Biochemistry, with her mom. We hug, I return the light pleasantries, and wisely return to my corner. The hours come and go. The security guard approaches me, concerned about my lack of movement in the hours since I walked in.

"Excuse me, have you been attended to?"

I tell him I will be approaching the counter soon, but I am awaiting a phone call. He nods and walks away. I look up at the clock, it is now 2:50 pm, still no call, but I remain hopeful. Mom did say I would hear from her, plus there was the time difference to factor in. I ignore the guard's confronting stares and wait in silence. Moments later, my phone rings. This time, it's my buddy, Sylvia. She was done with classes for the day and wondered where I was. She promised to let me copy her notes whenever I was ready. I thank her and tell her I will catch her later, freeing up my line in case the long-awaited call came in.

I glance at the clock again; it's now 3:23pm. The bank would close in precisely 37 minutes, taking with it any dreams I had of joining the 2009 graduating class and still no call from Mom. The bank's AC is on, but I'm sweating profusely, the cold air doing nothing for my increasing anxiety.

The security guard walks over again, "Since you are not on the queue, perhaps you stand here at the side so that those seeing the teller can sit, okay?"

I graciously stand, ignoring the prying eyes across the hall. It's now 3:50pm. The banking hall began to gradually clear out. Just a handful of people were left waiting to see the tellers. This time, the Branch Manager herself walks over to me:

"Young lady, is there anything I can help you with? Would you like to speak privately in my office? You've been here for hours without performing a transaction. Is there anything I can do for you?"

I assure her that everything is okay and that I would be approaching the counter shortly. She reminds me that the bank closes in 10 minutes, and like a supermodel in ash gray Neiman Marcus and wedge pumps, she primly catwalks back into her lavish office. The clock hits 4:00pm. The security guard, keys in hand, returns, this time, politely asking me to leave. The bank was officially closed. He advised that I come back on Monday. For me, that was not an option. My lips tremble, my cheeks flush. I glance randomly across the room, so is this really how it ends? I end up deferring the year?

I reluctantly stand. Teary-eyed, with sweaty palms and moist hairline, shoulders downcast.

Just then, the phone rings. Mom gives me the details of the transfer. I rush to the teller, who was now rounding up for the day.

"Sir, please, today is the final day for registration. I know you are closed, but I really need your help to make just one transaction. I need you to please, please, payout this cash, convert it to US dollars, and deposit it into the University's account. I have to do this TODAY."

He stands up, turning to leave, mumbling something about not having eaten all day. The matronly Branch Manager, sensing my desperation, intervenes, instructing all three tellers to help me.

By 4:28pm, the required $6,000 of my outstanding fees were miraculously paid. I had just 32 minutes left to get to Great Hall to finalize my registration. Given the rush-hour crowd on campus, all the taxis passing were occupied.

I ran halfway, panting along the way; I made it to the administration block at 4:50, only to see the registrar strolling to her car with her 10-year-old daughter, set for an early start to the weekend. I rushed to her, pleading for a chance to get my name on the list. Her displeasure was evident. She half-heartedly returned to her office and restarted her PC. She reviewed my receipts, double-checked the spelling of my name and index number, and typed them in.

Just as she hit the "enter" key on her keyboard, the clock struck 5:00, the University's registration system closed.

I was the very last person to register that day. Don't tell me miracles don't happen!

Humbled by the emotional crests and troughs of the day, I gratefully hug the registrar and thank her for her support. It is easy to remember that day because, on August 22, I got to see the hand of God at work. In school, as with many other life events to come, I would be the last to register, last to arrive, last to enroll, last to start, and sometimes even last to finish.

In 2005, I arrived at the University of Ghana several weeks into the 1st semester of my freshman year after resigning from my job in Voinjama because my admission letter arrived late. So, I had to catch up. As I struggled to raise fees to stay in school over the years, I would be late in starting class with the others. Again, I would have to catch up. I seemed to somehow make it through just in the nick of time. That, dear reader, is my backstory.

From August 2008, for two semesters in a row, I managed to register just in time, on the very last day, ending up as the very last name on the student roster, but none of that mattered. I made the cut.

The older I get, the more I find myself drawn to books, movies, and documentaries based on true-life stories and actual events because they give you a glimpse into the backstory. It is one thing to hear the summary of a person's success; it's another to be invited into their backstory. Behind every bio is a story of highs and lows, successes and failures, tears and triumphs. To regard an individual without an appreciation for the process it took him/her to get there is a disservice to the entirety of a person's lived experience.

***

Beyond the army of parents, aunts, uncles, and family members who helped steer my ship through college into life, there were also many non-relations, people I did not know from Adam who entered my life and provided anchorage along the way. I owe a lot to these "Josephs of Arimathaea," who showed up at the right time when I needed it the most. Figuratively, *Joseph of Arimathaea* is someone you perhaps did not know who steps onto the scene to help you progress on life's journey.

In Biblical tradition[62], Joseph of Arimathea shows up after Jesus' crucifixion and offers up his very own reserved tomb for Jesus' body to be buried in. Not much else is mentioned about him apart from the fact that he was a wealthy member of society. Yet, he shows up, powerfully influential, just in time, and salvages the situation.

On my Legon journey, Dr. Frederick Phillips and Mr. John Egyir-Croffet were my "Josephs of Arimathaea." Dr. Phillips provided extra Chemistry lessons, moral support, and encouragement to help me succeed in school. Mr. Croffet lobbied as much as he could to ensure I stayed in school. Dr. Phillips was my inorganic chemistry professor; I met him in my 1st year during registration for CHEM 101. His 2nd year course, CHEM 201 Inorganic Chemistry, was the only course I outright flunked and had to repeat during my four years in Legon.

After months of dedicated studies, I got a disturbing call from Liberia moments before my CHEM 201 exam, informing me that Dad had been rushed to the hospital. And so, just like that, all my carefully crammed formulas vanished into thin air as I entered the exam hall. Of course, the outcome was disastrous. I failed miserably. Concerned about how my grades had tanked in the exam compared to mid-term, Dr. Phillips, with three college-age children himself, stepped in, offering make-up lessons, fatherly advice, and moral support. His campus home and lovely wife, Aunty Agnes, were a haven for delicious Sunday meals.

Mr. John Egyir-Croffet was the Student Counselor of the University of Ghana. Students went to see him for everything from family problems, issues in their love-life, challenges with grades, deferment of the school year, and support in approaching the University on financial aid. When Dad fell ill and things started to go south, I went to see him for assistance to withdraw from the University. As Lee Ann Womack cautions against in her song, *"I Hope You Dance,"* I was choosing *"the path with least resistance."* I was taking the easy way out; I could not see my way to the finish. Mr. Croffet took one good look at me and decided that that was out of the question.

He set out on a personal mission to ensure I stayed in and graduated from the University of Ghana. He wrote letters to Ecobank, Ideal College[w], and countless others on my behalf. He even wrote to the school requesting they grant me more time to raise funds. As an international student, it took much lobbying to mobilize just fractions of my tuition, but Mr. Croffet never gave up and would not let me. His rugged faith, optimism, and youthful demeanor kept spurring me on in what seemed like a hopeless adventure. Still, Mr. Croffet left no stone unturned.

When massive efforts had been made, and the funds still fell short in my final semester, he and his wife did something I will never forget. They emptied their accounts and paid off whatever was left of my tuition. I stood in the bank, weeping in disbelief as this couple took such an audacious

w The author wishes to acknowledge and wholeheartedly thank Ecobank Ghana Limited and Ideal College Legon for their financial contributions in advancing her career aspirations.

bet on my future.

"No, Mr. Croffet, I can't let you do this, please." I tearfully pleaded.

"You are our daughter, Magdalene. We may not have been blessed with biological children. Still, you are our daughter, let us do this for you," Mr. Croffet insisted, as I unsuccessfully tried to dissuade him from cashing out his family's savings on my account.

He did it anyway.

For as long as I live, I will never forget Mr. John Egyir-Croffet or the lengths he went to ensure I clutched my Bachelor's Degree from the prestigious University of Ghana. My Legon story, my life story, can never be written without recollecting his invaluable input.

For years, my parents had invested in and so generously helped so many people. Life sometimes has a peculiar way of returning the goodwill. I share this all to say, no one makes it on his or her own. Someone encouraged you, helped raise funds on your behalf, cooked for you, tutored you, believed in you. Someone stood beside the boxing ring of life, cheering, spurring you on to fight another round when you were ready to throw in the towel and hand in your gloves. Those ingredients merged to make you the woman or man you are today. Someone gave you a hand up. Never forget that. Whenever you have the chance, pay it forward. You, too, can be an outstretched arm helping to lift another. You also can be a "Joseph of Arimathaea" to someone else along life's journey.

***

Legon will always hold a special place in my heart. As much as it was a sanctuary of growth and learning, it was also a

142

place of loss. My toughest hurdle in college was overcoming Dad's passing at the beginning of my 3rd year. I was most definitely a Daddy's girl to the bone, which is why losing my father the year I turned 20 has been the most enduring loss of my life.

During that time of mourning, I would take solitary evening walks through the Legon Hills' serene environs, near the illustrious Faculty residences. I would walk for miles, near the famous Sarbah Field, where tens of students gathered daily to pray. There, I would meditate, reflect, cry a bit, then cry some more, trying to piece together the fragments of my broken heart. You see, grief has a way of surprising you. It shakes you to the core, cuts you open, and leaves you to stitch yourself back up, however best you can.

On these walks alone, surrounded by the echoes of prayer, I would pour out my broken heart to God—my audience of One, either in prayer or song. It was during one of those peaceful moments of reading and meditation that I stumbled across an inspiring story that would come to mean so much to me on my journey to healing.

The story is told of five sisters, Mahlah, Noah, Hoglah, Milkah, and Tirzah, Mr. Zelophehad's daughters[63]. Their father dies at the end of Israel's 40-year exodus from Egypt through the wilderness into Canaan, leaving the girls orphaned. Customarily, they had no right to inheritance, given their gender. Still, these daring sisters went before Moses, leader of the people at the time, and, in a historically unprecedented move, courageously petition him to grant them property rights among their father's relatives. To paraphrase, they were asking:

> *"What happens to us now that our father is dead and left no son?"*

What happens to fatherless girls in a world where property rights are reserved only for men? What happens to us since we have no brothers to inherit on our behalf? What happens to us, seeing that our gender disqualifies us from the right of inheritance? As a nation under theocratic rule, Moses confers with God on behalf of Zelophehad's daughters. God's reply is fascinating:

> *"What Zelophehad's daughters are saying is right. You must give them property as an inheritance among their father's relatives and give their father's inheritance to them."*

What follows is even more mind-blowing. As the story goes, the nation's inheritance laws, basically Israel's constitution, were amended to accommodate the five women's plight. Mahlah, Noah, Hoglah, Milkah, and Tirzah wove their way into land ownership in a time when the original land tenure laws clearly made no provisions for women.

"What happens to us?" is a question that would stick with me for years to come. What happens to fatherless girls that seem to be getting lost in a torrential world? They survive. That was the comfort I held onto to sail through my remaining college semesters but also to navigate life.

When I returned to school in Ghana after the funeral in Liberia in September 2007, it was very hard grieving Dad away from home, distant from my family, especially since all my friends still had the comfort of fatherly wisdom and protection. Meanwhile, as grief-stricken as I was, life did offer a silver lining. That year, my classmates voted me in as Class Representative, which they would unanimously insist I remain from 3rd year straight up to graduation. The increased responsibility of that liaison role between the Faculty and students helped redirect my focus from my heartache to responding to the needs of my other 62 classmates. What a father represents in his daughter's life is far more than words could ever fully articulate. Nigerian Novelist Chimamanda Adichie, sharing her emotions on the recent passing of her own father, writes:

> *"Grief is a cruel kind of education. You learn how ungentle mourning can be, how full of anger. You learn that your side muscles will ache painfully from days of crying. You learn how glib condolences can feel.[64]"*

Losing Dad was a grim tunnel that took me years to crawl my way out of. I miss him every single day, especially at significant life events: at graduations, when it was time to march down the aisle on my wedding day, giving birth to the kids, and now at the release of this book. I grieved deeply not just because of what I knew I had lost in losing my father, but because of what I knew many others lost with his passing.

To thousands of people, Gabriel Baccus Matthews was the embodiment of indigenous political consciousness, their anticipated seat at the table, their bridge to socio-economic inclusion, their aspiration for a better Liberia. His passing represented hope deferred to these people—the dimming of a torch lit in their youth as far back as the 1970s.

I mourned for him, but I also grieved for them. I grieved for the hundreds that had relentlessly followed him their entire adult lives, faithfully serving in the United People's Party (UPP) as bodyguards, supporters, mobilizers, and party stalwarts. The people who believed that somehow, this romance between Dad and Liberia would still someday be.

When Dad fell ill, they, like us, had all nursed the belief that it could not possibly be the end. Sadly, it was, leaving us all with the burden of continuing on life's road without him.

***

My journey through the University of Ghana was laced with many speedbumps, potholes, and manholes. From challenges raising fees to health scares, Dad's battle with cancer, and his eventual passing at the start of my 3rd year.

Still, on November 7, 2009, I graduated 1st in my class, valedictorian of the University of Ghana's Department of Animal Biology and Conservation Science[x], with the highest CGPA[y]; because in life, it does not matter how you start or what you endure in the process, it is how you finish that counts.

Indian Poet, Vinati Bhola, captures it so beautifully:

> *"i was not born with roses*
> *in my chest*
> *to be afraid of thorns.*
> *i was born to*
> *bloom*
> *in spite of them[65]."*

No matter what life brings, it is still possible to bloom in spite of the thorns.

So don't you dare give up.

---

x Formerly Zoology Department
y Cumulative Grade Point Average

Chapter 7

Mediterranean Sunsets

"But I know, somehow, that only when it is dark enough can you see the stars[66]."

Martin Luther King, Jr, US Civil Rights Icon

The year 2012 will always represent a pivotal moment in my life. Contrary to what Nostradamus predicted, the world did not come to an end that year, and it proved to be one of the best years of my life. It was the year I turned 25. The year I finished graduate school, got selected for my first trip to an international conference outside Africa, released my first book, and won an award for my graduate dissertation. It was one year; I will always remember.

In September 2011, I traveled to Cyprus to attend the Harvard Cyprus Institute for Environmental and Public Health on a full scholarship to pursue a Masters in Environmental Health. The institute was located in the charming Cypriot city of Limassol.

The island of Cyprus is a stunning place. From its idyllic location on the Mediterranean Sea, just a stone throw away from Greece, the Middle East, and Europe, its characteristic topography and rich history, schooling in Cyprus was as much cultural immersion as intellectual. The tranquil beaches in Protaras, the mythical Aphrodite rock in Pafos, the chilly hills of the ancient Trodos & Kykkos Monastery were all memorable landmarks I had the privilege to visit. The Cypriot population was predominantly aged; the young people tend to travel to Europe and the United Kingdom to make life, returning to the island to retire and enjoy the relaxed pace of life and the fantastic Mediterranean weather.

As I was settling into my exotic surroundings and adjusting to being back in the classroom, tragedy struck just days after my arrival. I received the heartbreaking call from Martin that our brother Andrew had been killed in a car accident on his way home from church that September 11th. Martin cautioned that I stay away from Facebook as condolence messages were already pouring in long before Andrew's siblings and family even got the news. I just have to say, these over-zealous people that see the need to announce a person's passing on social media before the family even has a chance to reach immediate relations never cease to amaze me. Upon hearing the news, I was devastated.

I had spoken to Andrew just a few days before, on the 4th anniversary of our father's passing. Hearing he, too, had passed was a real shock. I was starting a new school year in a strange city surrounded by people I barely knew. How do you process such a loss and stay focused on producing the grades required to maintain your scholarship? How does a person cope?

In their seminal work, *On Grief and Grieving,* Elizabeth Kubler-Ross and David Kessler argue that, as humans, we encounter grief in five stages. We experience a bit of denial, anger, bargaining, depression, and, eventually, acceptance. They hypothesize that while the sequence is purely descriptive, the stages may occur one after another in some cases and in others somewhat simultaneously. Each person's journey is unique, and the acceptance stage sometimes takes a while to arrive at. With Andrew's passing merely four years after Dad's, at the same time of year, it only served to deepen the wound, leaving me in a blurry haze.

Since I was only a few weeks into the school year, I explored options to defer the year, but something deep inside me wanted to fight it out as I had done when Dad passed back in college. I knew it would be hard, but I also knew I had to at least try. Both Dad and Andrew would have wanted me to. Still, once again, it was tough, extremely tough. In the wisdom of school policy, my professors recommended I take up sessions with the University's Counselor to help me better cope. Since Mr. Croffet, that would turn out to be my second encounter with structured counseling, again facilitated by my academic institution.

***

Ms. Iliana Stylianou[z], the school's counselor, was a gorgeous blonde with dancing hazel eyes and a chiseled, model-like jawline. With her vibrant fashion sense and impeccable make-up, she came for sessions looking like someone who had just stepped off a Parisian runway to do community service. Yet, neither her neon pink gel manicure nor framed wall-mounted credentials could have prepared her for her first meeting with me. You see, in Western culture, grief can be polished. It is this well-packaged expression of emotion, concealed under dark shades and a black-veiled fascinator à la Celine Dion, or the "stiff upper-lip demeanor" required of Princes William and Harry as they escorted Princess

---

z Not her real name.

Diana's coffin to Westminster Abbey.

In Africa, mourning is expressed across a spectrum. It can be anything from shocked, silent tears to endless sobs, shouts, screams, and even attempts at rolling on the floor. There is no such thing as too much, no expectation of propriety, and absolutely no efforts made at concealing the enormous, messy emotions being felt.

Religion and culture permitting, you can grieve a lost loved one in whatever form you see best. In fact, you are expected to mourn visibly; anything short of that, in some contexts, would raise grave suspicion of superstitious foul play.

Conscious of my surroundings, I kept staving off the urge to cry before this elegant woman, but she was persistent. She sat down next to me with a box of Kleenex and went on probing and prodding at my wounded heart, peeling away at the scabs, appealing to my vulnerability, wanting me to "feel." When I finally let go, allowing myself to "feel," I burst into the most shocking tears she had ever seen! The dam of propriety broke, and years of pent-up, unspoken pain gushed their way out.

The loss of Dad, Andrew, my older buddy, Beatrice Toe, to an unexplained illness, other friends, and close relatives. The loss of my innocence. Surviving childhood abuse. Living through traumatic years of war. Living up to the expectations of having to step in to help care for older ailing relatives, including Dad, during his cancer battle. Coping with the pressures of having to be strong for years when all I wanted to do was curl up, and die, disappear, runaway, escape my life.

Years of unconfronted grief came rushing out. I wept so intensely and so achingly, it left Ms. Stylianou completely confused! She did not know whether to hug me, hold me, or just stare on in disbelief! She opted to just let me cry my heart out. By the time I was done sobbing, 45 minutes had passed, our first session was over! Stunned by my outburst, she went on to say:

"Wow! I admire how in-tune you are with your feelings. I'm sure you feel much better now?"

I smiled, visibly relieved of a heavy burden; I quietly nodded. Ms. Stylianou smiled back, pleased to have made "progress" with her new client. "Let's do this again next Friday, same time, okay?"

This time, we both laughed, shook hands, and I, consoled, walked a lot happier out the door.

Jamie Anderson once said,

> *"Grief, I've learned, is really just love. It's all the love you want to give but cannot. All that unspent love gathers up in the corners of your eyes, the lump in your throat, and in that hollow part of your chest. Grief is just love with no place to go[67]."*

Having just landed in Cyprus, I couldn't afford another trip back to the US to attend Andrew's funeral. I watched the ceremony virtually, crying alone, thousands of miles away from home, with no one to hug, no familiar hand to hold. I certainly had a lot of love-filled grief that had no place to go. The counseling sessions became my outlet.

Counseling isn't everyone's cup of tea; I get that. Not everyone is comfortable airing their vulnerabilities to some random stranger. Meanwhile, from my experience, I found the act of seeking professional help after life's losses to be extremely helpful. It provided me with a judgment-free zone to:

a) unleash my deepest feelings, and

b) share my darkest truths without having to worry about being politically correct, analyzing the pitch of how my thoughts would come across, or overthinking whose feelings might be hurt by what I would say.

In those counseling sessions, I could finally speak my mind. FREELY. That, for me, was cathartic. I could cry if I needed to, vent if I had to, and do all of this with the help of a trained professional who would embrace my painful meltdowns and help me make sense of the myriad of messy emotions I was feeling. The closest analogy I can give for my time with Iliana is like a visit to the Doctor. You detail all your symptoms and allow yourself to be examined. The Doctor then prescribes the right course of action/medication to address your ailment. Being able to talk about my various lived experiences in a judgment-free zone has been one of the most essential steps in my healing journey in recent years. Because you see, some seasons of life can be tough. As my God-brother Romeo Clarke puts it:

"Life is never black and white. There are so many colors, and then there are 50 shades of gray."

So how do you navigate this life without losing your mind? He adds: *Learn to color, and live."* Some of us have been through so much adversity in this thing called life that our emotional shock absorbers have literally worn out. We have no option but to stay strong, never complain, keep going, regardless of what we feel or face. But you see, every now and then in battle, even the fiercest warriors need to have their wounds nursed before returning to action.

Despite the uphill climb, my year in Cyprus would be one of the most productive years of my life. I obtained my Masters in Environmental Health from the reputable Harvard School of Public Health's Cyprus International Institute.

I completed the manuscript for my first book, RISE! I invested time in researching for and writing an essay on lead exposure in children in sub-Saharan Africa. That essay was later selected as one of the top 100 essay entries at the 43rd St. Gallen Symposium in Switzerland, securing me an all-expense-paid trip to attend the symposium and engage with other graduate students from around the world. I did all this with tears in my eyes, silently grieving the loss of my big brother.

As Matthews siblings, Andrew represented what was best in all of us. He was brilliant, funny, and outrageously quiet. You could sit with him in a room for hours, and he would just be there, a reassuring presence, smiling tenderly at you without saying a word. It was Andrew who taught me square root in Math and helped me make sense of 8th grade Algebra. He was the only person I knew who could do long division in his head down to decimals in a matter of seconds without a calculator. He loved to dance and would often beat me at video games. As children growing up, he would share his deep interest in Microbiology and dreams of someday being the first researcher to find the cure for HIV/AIDS. Losing him so tragically and so untimely would significantly affect my other brothers and me, with each of us responding to it in our own way.

For some, that was the last straw that toppled their fledgling religious beliefs. For others, it was the spark that drove them to try harder, work smarter in his memory, and make the most of this fleeting thing called life. As for me, for months after that, I would wake up each day reciting:

"If you have run with the footmen, and they have wearied you, then how can you contend with horses?[68]*"*

The analogy of confronting horses versus footmen in life's

journey would serve as my daily inspiration to keep striving for what was ahead across changing times and seasons. In life's losses, I would come to fully comprehend the depth of author Jodi Picoult's words,

> *"The human capacity for burden is like bamboo far more flexible than you'd ever believe at first glance[69]."*

Following the grief theory, I have come to realize that when it comes to grief or loss like the passing of a loved one or sexual and emotional abuse, we tend to start off in denial, burying the occurrence into our subconscious to escape the reality unfolding within and around us. When we finally come to a place of acknowledgment, sometimes there's a bit of anger, anger at God, anger at our parents, anger at our abusers, anger at ourselves, anger at the world—a deep-seated rage boiling on the inside of us. In the shadows of that rage, some people move on to bargaining. We dive into this stage of endless "If only..." and "What if..." statements. We wish to go back into time, undo what has been done, erase what has been etched, resurrect that which has died.

If only we had called our parents and siblings more. If only we had said "I love you" more. If only we had been more careful, more prudent, more cautious, if only we had fought harder, screamed louder, said something to someone, gone to the authorities. If only we had not been so afraid of the stigma, afraid to be maligned, afraid of public opinion, afraid of society's reaction. Drowning in guilt, this stage is one of regret and pain in which we wish we had done everything differently. In this court, where guilt hangs supreme as judge, jury, and executioner, we tend to blame ourselves, fault ourselves, try ourselves, and eventually sentence ourselves.

"I should have ended the call with I love you. Heck, from

now on, I will end every call to friends and family with "I love you."

"Of course, it was my fault; I went over to his house."

"I let him into the house. I didn't scream loud enough."

We replay scenes over and over in our minds, convinced beyond all reasonable doubt that we are indeed guilty. Meanwhile, our present is arrested in the past as we struggle to negotiate our way out of the hurt. Then, when we are not careful, depression comes rushing in. Repeated cycles of depression lay hold before we finally make it to that place of acceptance—that place where we neither feel okay or alright about the loss in our lives, but we somehow make peace with it. We choose to learn to live with it, recognizing that this new reality, however painful it may be, is now the new normal, a new bittersweet fact of life.

We may never like this reality, nor will it ever be okay, but with time, after much tears, pain, and regret, eventually, we accept it. We learn to live in a world where our hearts are broken, our innocence taken, our loved one is missing, our soul—our glassy sculptured soul is shattered. Acceptance and closure lie at the end of the tunnel if only we would be courageous enough to brave the storms to get there.

***

As I added finishing touches to this manuscript, something happened on the global stage that sadly reminded me of another layer to life in Cyprus that went beyond the island's exquisite sunsets, historical heritage, and the professional and emotional strides I made while schooling there. It was 2020, and the world was faced with a one-in-a-century public health pandemic, the COVID-19 outbreak. At the peak of the pandemic, nations had shut down for weeks, economies stood still as millions of people across Asia, Europe, Africa, and the Americas sheltered in place to lessen the spread of the virus and hopefully flatten the skyrocketing epidemiological curve. By June 2020, the world had hit 8.7 million confirmed cases and nearly half a million deaths[70].

As preventive measures such as handwashing, wearing masks, and practicing social distance, yielded some positive outcomes, major cities worldwide gradually reopened. Just as authorities began implementing a phased approach to open restaurants, barbershops, and retail centers, something else happened.

Another black man died at the hands of a white police officer in broad daylight. This time, the video surfaced of George Floyd being killed a slow, gut-wrenching death as Officer Derek Chauvin pushed him down against the pavement with his knee forcefully pressed into Floyd's neck for nearly 10 whole minutes. The 42-year-old, towering 6'7" Floyd begged for his life, under Officer Chauvin's knee, to the point of crying out for his mother, while two other officers mercilessly pinned him down, and another stood by complicit till he breathed his last. A courageous 17-year-old girl on the scene captured it all on video. It was such a gruesome video that once you saw it, you could never unsee. Floyd's alleged crime for which he was being arrested was non-lethal. He purportedly made a purchase with a counterfeit $20 bill. The procedure required the shop owner to phone the police, but it certainly did not call for killing an unarmed, handcuffed man.

The sheer cruelty with which George Floyd succumbed on a Minneapolis street corner broke millions of hearts and sent disturbing shockwaves around the world. Two days later, when County Officials failed to arrest Chauvin or any of the other officers involved, people took to the streets. Protests erupted in every major city in the US, with people of all ages and races taking to the streets to demand justice and end systemic racism.

At its highest moments, in some states, the protests were tearful, deeply moving scenes in which police officers apologized for the grave wrong done by some of theirs, with hundreds of officers taking a knee in solidarity with the protesters. At its lowest, the protests were violent, involving heated exchanges with riot police, stones, pepper spray, rubber bullets, flash-bangs, property damage, human casualties, and looting of stores.

It was a harrowing moment in history, one that triggered every black person around the world to the core. I watched the video, weeping profusely. I saw it just once and could not bring myself to watch it again. George Floyd's face, violently pressed against the pavement, represented millions of black faces around the world. I pictured my husband, whose sense of adventure and interest in architecture sometimes takes him on drives in very white neighborhoods, where he would be the only black person.

I pictured my 27-year-old, 200lb baby brother, who, no matter how much muscles he has built over the years from playing high school football, will still be the hazel-eyed baby I used to tickle. My heart pounds faster as I think of my own 3-year-old black son. My precious boy, whose only request on any given day is to go to the playground; is this the world he is to grow up in? Emotions rise, my hands shake, my lips tremble.

Watching the Floyd footage, I tearfully recollected my own bitter taste of racism. My mind wandered to Cyprus, the blissfully beautiful Mediterranean island, where I spent a year attending graduate school. Schooling in Cyprus meant living in a place where I would be a minority for the first time in my adult life. We were just three black students in the Harvard Cyprus Program. Benedicta, from Ghana, along with Moses and me from Liberia. We were all on full scholarships and were flatmates, residing in the Program's allocated housing for its scholars. We were warmly nicknamed "the African contingent" by our friend, Nazrul, from Bangladesh.

Looking back, I remember how our neighbor from down the street would tighten her grip on her kids whenever she saw us walking home from class.

"What on earth would we possibly do to her kids?" I quipped.

I recall one day when a lady dashed down the block in high heels, rushing into her car, frantically winding up her windows and locking her doors in fear of us. More upsettingly, I remember how the men would call out derogatory "20 euros" catcalls each time they saw Benedicta and me walking through the streets of Limassol. An elderly man in his 60s once flung open his bathrobe from the 1st-floor balcony of his apartment, revealing his nude genitals in broad daylight to entice us to join him upstairs. Shocked, we could not believe our eyes. Somehow our huge epidemiology and statistics textbooks were not enough indications that we were students. We were there on full merit-based Harvard School of Public Health Scholarships, but none of that mattered. Feeding into the stereotype, as young black women on a historically white island, we could only be there "on business," trading the goods and services of our curvy, Nubian bodies. I had never felt so insulted, so humiliated, so denigrated as a black woman.

Then came the older folks, that silver-haired racism—the type so generationally ingrained that it pays no mind to any form of contemporary political correctness. We were walking home from Starbucks after studying Biostatistics one lovely Sunday afternoon, and here comes this elderly lady, in her seventies, walking up behind us at the traffic light. Benny and I exchanged girly giggles while checking out the new items on sale through the GAP display window across the street. That's when we hear a raised voice right behind us:

"Hey, Black... Black! You, Black! Move! Move! Shoo! Shoo!" With a trembling hand and shriveled spine, she was using her metallic cane to shoo us away as you would little dogs.

The energy of the moment dissipated. As old and frail as this lady was, she still had enough strength to spew racist slurs. Unbelievable! We were too stunned to respond. African culture teaches respect for elders, but racism is where we draw the line. We decided we would not move. She would have to wait her turn. The light turned red, the cars came to a halt, and we majestically crossed the street. We were not puppies and would not be treated as such. Again, few days to Christmas 2011, Benny and I were window shopping along the famous Anexartisias street in downtown Limassol, when a rowdy guy, in a ruby red, convertible SL500, slowed down and shouted "I like chocolate!" while performing sexually explicit mouth gestures.

As intellectually enriching as it was, my one year of grad school in Cyprus was socially-deprecating. The men thought we were prostitutes. The elderly, whose interactions with black people were mostly as domestic help, treated us as inferiors. Thankfully, the younger generation was more cosmopolitan. They had traveled and experienced other cultures; they were more welcoming. I guess that is what happens when a person spends his/her entire life on an island in this fictitious bubble with your own kind, where you are taught to believe that anything foreign is inferior.

Never before had my race mattered as it did in grad school. Benny and I held our breath through that year, and although we loved the breathtaking scenery and Mediterranean sunsets, we were just as eager to return to the motherland, to the sweet taste of home.

People shy away from the topic of racism because it makes them uncomfortable. To some, it is overrated; to others, it is one of those things that the less said, the better. But how can you just cast a blind eye on the harrowing lived experience of an entire race of people around the world? To discuss racism is to acknowledge that black people have historically been and continue to be treated unjustly in many parts of the world. But the discourse must transcend mere acknowledgment to action. How do we fix it? How can people of other races become more self-aware in their relationship with people of the black race? How can nations function and leaders govern equitably in administering healthcare, social services, policing, and access to justice for all citizens? How do we stop what happened to George Floyd from happening to anyone else?

According to the Universal Declaration of Human Rights, which Pope John Paul II once called *"one of the highest expressions of the human conscience of our time[71],"*

> *"All human beings are born free and equal in dignity and rights. They are endowed with reason and conscience and should act towards one another in a spirit of brotherhood[72]."*

Still, the concept of equality "in dignity and rights" remains elusive in many parts of the world. As Dr. Martin Luther King said:

> *"We have learned to fly the air like birds and swim the sea like fish, but we have not learned the simple art of living together as brothers[73]."*

At the close of the school year, when the Institute's board asked me for my feedback on how they could improve the graduate experience for subsequent Fellows, my answer was simple. Academically, the program was excellent. The blend of a Harvard curriculum and world-class Faculty on the historic shores of the Mediterranean was an exceptional learning experience. What needed strengthening was the development of a more holistic, culturally-appropriate, gender-sensitive, and racially-conscious orientation package on the social and racial dynamics in Cyprus for African, Asian, or Middle Eastern students. This would be one step in helping lessen potential culture shocks during their stay.

***

Despite everything happening in and around me, I still graduated in the top tier of my class. It was 19th-century writer Washington Irving that said:

> *"There is in every true woman's heart, a spark of heavenly fire, which lies dormant in the broad daylight of prosperity, but which kindles up and beams and blazes in the dark hour of adversity[74]."*

In grad school, as with college, with my brother's passing as with Dad's, somehow, I managed to pull through adversity and graduate with Honors. Once again, blooming despite the thorns.

As Paulo Coelho so powerfully writes in the classic novel, *The Alchemist,*

> *"Before a dream is realized, the Soul of the World tests everything that was learned along the way. It does this not because it is evil, but so that we can, in addition to realizing our dreams, master the lessons*

we've learned as we've moved toward that dream. That's the point at which most people give up. It's the point at which, as we say in the language of the desert, one 'dies of thirst just when the palm trees have appeared on the horizon[75]."

That year, I also found myself overwhelmed by the insistent desire to contribute to the youth in my country Liberia. Beyond my professional WASH portfolio, I set out to write a book that would answer the many questions young Liberians had about life. Sure, there were many self-help resources on the market that anyone could purchase; but our socioeconomics and geo-politics were worlds apart from the western countries where most of those books were written. It had to be crafted after the unique dynamics of our post-conflict, national recovery.

With the pronounced lack of structured career guidance and mentorship in most schools, I chose to write a nationally-relevant and culturally-appropriate resource that would offer guidance counseling in a book. In between classes and dissertation research, I dedicated my free time to writing and compiling insights around essential life skills, job-hunting, scholarship searching, and entrepreneurial development tailored to the peculiarities of the Liberian context. I later released *RISE! Redeeming the Future of Liberia, a Practical Guide to Self-Development*. It was well-received by many young people and learning institutions across Liberia. The Minister of Education at the time, Honorable Etmonia Tarpeh, would refer to RISE writing the following:

"As the nation strives to attain middle-income status by 2030, it is our sincere desire that this valuable resource is disseminated more widely in high schools, universities, and graduate schools across the country."

After completing grad school, I made it a point to host seminars and motivational talks at various high schools and colleges across Liberia, all centered on helping young people make more informed choices about their lives and future.

Youth empowerment, girls' upliftment, and the advancement of STEM (Science, Technology, Engineering, and Maths) education remain passionate interests I hold dear. By writing books, conducting applied research, or supporting projects in development work, my dream is to continue contributing to sustainable development in Africa and uplifting Mama Liberia in whichever way I can.

For every glimmer of success there has ever been in my life, every inch of progress, it has not been without its share of friction, resistance, and many high tides to cross. I have had to jump through many hoops and scale many walls. But despite the enormous, sometimes even heart-breaking challenges, I have stayed the course and kept on striving.

I used to think that life was all about the destination, getting from point A to point B. I have learned that life is as much about the destination as it is about the journey.

In the inspiring words of my Godmother Nomor Clarke, *"Life is a process, and not an event."*

It is as much about the mountaintop moments as the many valleys and cliffs you scale to get there. Now, I make it a point to enjoy the journey and take in the scenery as I go, despite the speedbumps along the way.

SECTION 3

LOVE

Sonnet 29

When, in disgrace with fortune and men's eyes,

I all alone beweep my outcast state,

And trouble deaf heaven with my bootless cries,

And look upon myself and curse my fate,

Wishing me like to one more rich in hope,

Featured like him, like him with friends possessed,

Desiring this man's art and that man's scope,

With what I most enjoy contented least;

Yet in these thoughts myself almost despising,

Haply I think on thee, and then my state,

Like to the lark at break of day arising

From sullen earth sings hymns at heaven's gate;

For thy sweet love remembered such wealth brings

That then I scorn to change my state with kings[76]*.*

William Shakespeare

Chapter 8

The Womb of Time

"If we had no winter, the spring would not be so pleasant: if we did not sometimes taste of adversity, prosperity would not be so welcome[77]."

Anne Bradstreet, 17th Century American Poet

Liberia, 2013

It was Easter Sunday, 2013.

I quickly got dressed for church, eager to celebrate Resurrection Sunday, the most spectacular day of the Christian calendar. Good Friday Service two days before had been so fantastic, the Philadelphia Central Church Choir, that we lovingly called *"the #1 choir in the whole wide world,"* belted out one of my all-time favorites for the season, *The Work of the Blood.*

Today promised to only be more glorious. As I scaled the steep staircase at the church's entrance, all smiles, a male church member playfully came along with his iPad and abruptly took a picture with me. Caught off-guard, I politely smiled and quickly posed.

That was when she said it. So loud and calculating were her sentences:

"Mag-da-lene Mat-thews, when will we see yours? When-will-we-see-yours?" Her words were drawn out in syllables for effect.

"You keep posing and taking pictures with brothers— married brothers to share on Facebook. When will we see YOURS?"

The tone, timing, and pitch caused my hearty Easter Sunday smile to shrink to an embarrassed grin. Her words, though few, were fiery darts. To the people within earshot, climbing the steps at the time, I was being portrayed as that salacious single lady posing with the married men in church. As crushed as I was sitting through the service that day, it would take the charismatic message powerfully preached by Bishop George Harris to revive my shriveled spirit.

***

I find society is rather harsh on women—especially single women. I remember when I would show up at functions, and married women would tighten their grips around their husband's arms for fear of us single ladies in the room. Or when I would pay courtesy calls on some of my late father's friends, either just to keep in touch or request counsel on a matter, only to have the office staff assume I was their boss' latest arm candy. Now, on Easter Sunday, here I was named and shamed by—let's call her "Aunt Cora"—simply because I was a "SHE" and single.

Just for context, by this time in my life, one by one, my friends all seemed to be settling down. Once I got my masters and released my first book in the same year, what would have been a welcomed accomplishment in other parts of the world, only sparked more criticism as the awkward comments from older relations and "aunty figures" worsened. No woman needs to be reminded of the passing of time. Her own biological clock, coupled with the number of weddings and baby dedications she is invited to attend each month, are enough reminders. But to the people offering "loving advice" at the time, those were not loud enough. It had to be said. It had to be screamed. It had to be seasoned with a few teaspoons of salty public embarrassment so the message would sink.

You never really know what a person is going through. Coupled with external pressures, I dealt with internal challenges that seemed to be taking on a life of their own. After grad school, returning to Liberia brought me face to face yet again with the reality I had failed to confront. Social media had become a staple in everyone's daily experience. Facebook was a leading source of updates on trends and events happening around town. Sometimes while browsing leisurely, the picture of the man who robbed me of my innocence would pop up on my news feed. Instantly, my throat would run dry, my hands would shake, sweat would gather on my forehead, and like a horror movie on replay, that dreadful scene would flash afresh before my eyes.

For a split second, I would be 17 again, in that dark room, calling for help with no one in earshot, feeling helpless. I would hyperventilate, a downward emotional spiral would follow. For the next few days, I would become withdrawn, detached, in my own world, somewhat trapped in a dark tunnel, struggling to find my way to the light. Ironic, isn't it? This man was living his best life popping up on social media timelines, and here I was, several years later, still struggling to mend my shattered soul.

So, I did what most of us do to keep our minds off stuff: I kept busy. I channeled all my energies and emotions into work and service, and I really began excelling at it. To the outside world, I was really doing okay. It took me nearly a year of careful search after grad school, but I had finally landed my dream job in my preferred sector of water, sanitation, and hygiene.

I had the tremendous privilege of testing water and being paid to do it. For a lab nerd like me, it could not get better than that. I was young, female, hard-working, paid attention to detail, and got along well with everyone, from the MD to the plumber and the community chairperson. I brought in a unique skill set; I was an experienced water quality analyst and knew the ins and outs of physico-chemical, and microbial water testing. I knew if the water was safe to drink or not and, if it was not, what to do about it. I was high-achieving, meeting targets at work, delivering results, and helping to build something that would speak volumes in posterity.

At church, I was just as committed. I poured my heart and soul into leading the praise dance ministry, organizing worship evenings, training sessions, and workshops, helping to revolutionize dance as an art form in liturgical worship in Liberia. I also helped mentor teenage girls, getting them to make more prudent life decisions, trying my best to set a good example.

I ticked all the boxes of what a promising young woman was supposed to be. I graduated top of my class in both college and grad school and was trained by the best and brightest in the field of public health. On top of that, I had also become a published author by age 25. Professionally, I had finally settled in a niche in Liberia's tap water sector and began making a name for myself. I am sure my father was somewhere looking down at his little girl and smiling. As far as most of my family and friends were concerned, I had it together.

On the family front, I was doing my best to help with family responsibilities. I represented my family at weddings, meetings, and funerals. As is customary, I made sure Dad's gravesite was regularly cleaned and maintained. I helped relatives out financially and morally here and there. My paternal grandmother had moved back to Liberia, so, as the only and oldest granddaughter in the country, I was helping to keep an eye on both my Mom's mom and Dad's mom as best as I could. I did all this, but deep down, I was hurting. I was drowning emotionally, with recurring episodes of grim depression and very few people knew about it.

To "Aunt Cora's" point, of course, I wanted to "settle down and get married." But not without confronting the 400lb gorilla-sized ache in my soul. I needed to address unfinished business. I could not just get up and get married, putting someone through the arduous task of spending the rest of their life trying to "fix" me when I, myself, had not made serious attempts at getting fixed. I did want to settle down, but marriage scared me. With everything I had seen and was exposed to growing up, the expectation of fidelity from a spouse seemed foreign to me. I was not prepared to make such a crucial commitment without a brutal attempt to heal my unspoken hurt. I had lived with the secret of what had happened to me that fateful night for many years.

Yet, the closer I got to the decision of settling down and getting married, the more convinced I became of the need to unearth it and deal with it once and for all. It was like a bandaged wound that had not fully healed. It was time to yank the bandage off and let the wound heal in open air.

***

It was around this time that I shared my ordeal with my Mother for the very first time. Mind you, this was 10 years after it happened. In March 2014, Mom returned to Liberia to visit Grandma and me since her last visit during my college graduation in 2009. One day during her stay, I took her aside into my bedroom and, trembling, blurted out the truth that I had buried in my subconscious for so long. Mom wept, heartbroken by the magnitude of what I had shared. She held me close for what seemed like eternity, longing to comfort the ache that she now understood. On the grief spectrum, I had made it from denial to anger to recurring bouts of depression. By telling my Mom, I was now making my way through the stage of bargaining.

Time, they say, heals all wounds. I am of a different opinion. In my experience, time is merely anesthetic, numbing us to the reality of deep-seated, denied hurt that we would rather not feel. Healing is a process. It requires effort, intentionality, and resolve. Not a feeble hope that somehow, with the mystical passage of time, it will all go away. Much time had passed, and I was still hurting. I needed to find a balm to nurse the blistering wound in my soul. I needed to somehow grow into the best version of myself for anyone who was going *"to someday walk into my life and need someone to love them beyond reason.*[78]*"* I needed to heal for me, I needed to heal for him, I needed to heal for all the little angels who would someday call me "Mama," and young people who were looking to me for mentorship.

That year, to my utmost surprise, the day before my birthday, my friend and former classmate, Dennis, flew into Liberia from Ghana. He came to officially meet my mom and state his intentions for marriage. You know how they say, *"Once in a while, in the middle of an ordinary life, love gives us a fairy tale[79]?"* Well, it seems mine started to unfold.

The year before, while on maid-of-honor duties in Ghana for my best friend Sylvia's wedding, Dennis resurfaced in my life, purposefully, this time wanting to grow beyond friends. With everything I knew I was processing internally at the time, I dragged my feet, but he had made up his mind. Twelve months later, he was in Monrovia meeting my Mom and other family elders to convey his intentions about their daughter. The wheels fell into motion right after that.

You see, back in college, Dennis was one of the first persons to whom I entrusted the sordid details of my teenage experience. He was a great listener and a student pastor at the church where I fellowshipped then. Now that he had shared his intentions, I had hoped my "secret" would be a deterrent. I made sure to bring it up at every turn as a reason why he should consider another, but Dennis didn't care about any of that. He was determined to make me his wife. Pragmatist to the core, Dennis can sometimes take a while to act on stuff—very weighty in his decisions and actions. Oh! But when he does? You can never deter him after that!

Sadly, when you have been abused, such Jack-and-Rose-on-the-Titanic style love stories seem so far-fetched. Rape takes a toll on your self-esteem and femininity as a woman. You could spend many years believing that you are wasted goods, tainted, unworthy, undeserving of love if you are not careful. In my case, since 2004, the degrading line **"You are NOTHING"** continued to replay as background noise in my shattered soul, permeating my love life.

The one sacred space my abuser's sordid words did not touch was my self-confidence in my intellect. I knew I was smart. Heck, if there was anything I could take to the bank, it was my brains. The life-long reinforcement of good grades, class rankings, and awards had done their part to convince me of that much. With fair skin, sculpted legs, and 14-inch cascading hair, I knew I was attractive. Yet, I hesitated to trust any man without his own equally unflattering baggage, to love me enough to make me his wife, knowing full well what I had been through.

Dennis Ofori-Kuma was the very first person to look at me without judgment and say a liberating: *"I believe you."* In a "he said/she said" type situation where it is someone's word against yours, you long to be believed. You long to find another soul that knows and respects you well enough to understand and empathize with your truth. "I believe you" are words that could save a life. Three words that could set a soul free. Three words that would spell the difference between someone's past and future. Prisoners spend years writing to lawyers they do not know and detectives they have never seen, hoping that someone somewhere will finally believe in their innocence. Survivors of abuse spend years in silence until they find but one other soul genuine enough to accept their truth. Author Danielle Bernock writes:

> *"Trauma is personal. It does not disappear if it is not validated. When it is ignored or invalidated, the silent screams continue internally heard only by the one held captive. When someone enters the pain and hears the screams, healing can begin[80]."*

Despite all my reservations, Dennis entered my pain and encouraged me to find the strength to heal. I want to emphasize here that if you have lived through some form of abuse, it is essential to disclose your experience to a potential or current life partner. Full disclosure, trust, honesty, and communication are the bedrock to any lasting relationship. His/her support will go a long way on your road to closure. If you are serious about committing to this person, they have a right to know from the word go. There is always the fear that the person's feelings will change once they find out that you were "tainted." I get that because, for years, I, too, felt the same way. I used to be so unsure and insecure, especially in matters of the heart.

When a person genuinely loves you, your troubled past will not matter. He/she will enter your pain, stand by you, and move heaven and hell to ensure you get the help you need. They fight for your soul in the present so that you can live whole in the future, even if it means gutting out your shame in a book. That is what Dennis did for me. Where I had started on the journey, he stepped in and pushed me along through the dark tunnel of concealed pain into the light.

Unlike the passage of time, I have found that love, instead, is a more effective healer. Maya Angelou puts it like this:

> *"Love heals. Heals and liberates. I use the word love, not meaning sentimentality, but a condition so strong that it may be that which holds the stars in their heavenly positions and that which causes the blood to flow orderly in our veins[81]."*

Having been so hurt before, I struggled to unreservedly let love into my heart. But once I did, like Jennifer Elizabeth says, in *Born Ready*, it was like meeting *"a boy whose eyes showed me that the past, present, and future were all the same thing[82]."* The effect was electric. My negative poles seemed to have summoned his positivity somewhere out of the universe because he was everything I was not, but I was just right to him.

Where life dealt me a mixed hand of clubs, spades, hearts, and diamonds, Dennis' entire life could be summed up with a single card—the ace of spades. While my story was messy and melodramatic, shrouded by politics, war, and abuse, his was crisp and clean with minimal drama and damage. If our lives were music genres, mine would be Guns & Roses hard rock. Dennis' is definitely Kenny G's soothing jazz. I brought the bubbly ginger to his cool and calm.

Dennis would come to play a crucial role in my journey to inner healing. Where I struggled to swim through the sea of self-doubt and mixed emotions, he would toss me a life jacket of acceptance, one I held onto as I floated my way to the shores of closure.

***

Just when I thought I had enough reason to move past that horrific chapter, along came the kids whose bright eyes and endless smiles would motivate me daily to keep striving. My two little angels walked out of my dreams and into my life and irreversibly redefined my "why."

My children, Jordan and Mishan, have shown me a love I never knew existed. They love me—I did not have to be anything, do anything, or achieve anything. For me, that realization would be one of the most significant turning points in my quest for closure.

Motherhood would open a chapter for me that would forever change my life and perspective on just how far I am willing to go to be the best version of myself. A mother's love is something so pure, so breathtakingly beautiful, so priceless that it takes a woman herself to conceive and birth it into the world.

My entry into motherhood is a somewhat funny story; it happened after some 36 hours of labor. There I was covered in sweat on the morning of May 6, 2017. My mind, body, and soul were utterly exhausted; when the doctor handed me, my beautiful baby boy. My gaze quickly lands on the birthmark on his left cheekbone. Overwhelmed by emotions, tears well up in my eyes as he takes his first look at me, yawning. Our eyes lock, or so I thought. Time stood still. It was as if heaven was giving me a warm, comforting hug. For a moment, I could almost swear I heard the angelic host belting out the melodious "Hallelujah Chorus." My dreamy bonding moment with the little life in my arms came to a screeching halt as Dr. Hensley[aa] snapped me back to reality:

"You did such a great job, Mama. I'm going to finish getting you all cleaned up, so you feed the baby now, okay?"

I blinked twice in disbelief: "Doctor, say what now?"

After starving through a day and a half of labor, now that the baby was out, all I could picture was a hearty meal. I encouraged myself through contractions by imagining the 8 hours of sleep respite I would get at the end of the delivery-room tunnel. How come I had to get down to breastfeeding right away? "Couldn't we just put the baby to sleep and all get some much-needed rest after such torturous labor?" I wondered.

Nope, Mommy-duties called. I had to sit up, suck up all that post-partum pain, and give him what he needed the most at the time—nourishment. As I gently held his tender frame, I found myself slowly succumbing to the realization that it was no longer about me from here onwards.

In many cultures, it is believed:

> *"The moment a child is born, the mother is also born. She never existed before. The woman existed, but the mother, never[83]."*

---

aa Not her real name.

I had been given the sacred trust to conceive, carry, birth, and raise the generation that would follow. I had to live up to that. I was now a mother. Dennis and I share a hilarious laugh whenever we recall my rude awakening to motherhood. That call to nurture was my right of passage.

That day, Maggie as a Mother was born.

I reflect on my pregnancy journeys with a smile. Want to know what I am like as a pregnant woman? Picture a baleen whale struggling to float her way through to push-time. I am far from those Wonder Woman pregnant women on their feet till their due date, saving the world and rescuing kittens from fiery buildings. I'm no Lady Tarzan, taking on any jungles or striking yoga poses to strengthen my core. I am more your Humpty Dumpty kind of preggers. I go through the weeks and months like an exhausted mother hen waiting impatiently for her eggs to hatch.

Despite the unpleasantness of the journey—nausea, swollen feet, endless labs, doctor's visits, fatigue and waddle, absolutely nothing beats the outcome of the ride. One look in their glimmering eyes, and you have found the love of your life. A love that never existed until you birthed it into the world. A love so warm and divine that even the angels get jealous.

I owed it to myself and to this delicate life, snuggled in my arms to make sure I was healed and whole. I have in no way arrived at the finish line. I remain at it daily, but I wake up each day striving to be an inspiring epistle of healing for my children to someday read. Emerging phenom, Sarah Jakes Roberts, whose books and messages I so love, shares candid insights:

> *"I couldn't expect my infected soul to raise healthy children. I couldn't expect my insecurities to build*

a secure family. I couldn't stay shattered without breaking them. What if your life is the only manual on healing your children get to read? Who will they become? Children don't need perfection. They need genuine effort[84]."

Each day I make sure to keep pulling on that genuine effort. Some of you reading this might say, "Maggie, I am still struggling to heal; my story hasn't quite come together." Do not give up. Abuse may be short or long-term, but recovery takes a while. Go easy on yourself. The tears may be frequent, and the battles long. The questions may be more than the answers, and you hear the surly whispers that fade each time you show up in a gathering. That's okay.

You are going through an internal cleansing process, and as my buddy, Mitch Gopeya, says, *"Every time you clean something, you just make something else dirty."*

The dirt forced into your soul is being cleaned out. Believe me, you are making progress towards healing. Little by little, one step at a time, you will get there.

Pursuing emotional and psychological healing in the current state of the world can be daunting. The emotional pulse of the world as a whole is being stretched. Sarah Jakes puts it like this:

"So many of us are trying to navigate a today we've never seen while healing from a yesterday we can hardly understand[85]."

With a worldwide pandemic, glaring racial issues, socio-economic challenges, and the uncertainties of this new decade, as a global community, we are all *"trying to navigate a today we've never seen."* Life is not making much sense for many of us at this point. People are losing homes, livelihoods, and loved ones as a result of the pandemic. As survivors of abuse, we are trying to somehow pull through, striving to heal, saddled with hurt, learning to accept the apology we never got from our parents, assailants or people who deeply hurt us.

Even as I write this, I, too, am still not entirely where I had hoped to be at this point in my life. Then again, I gave up on elaborate life plans years ago, remember? As my mother would say, I am now more of a "one-day-at-a-time-sweet-Jesus" kind of girl, fueled by the loving promises of motherhood. My family remains the north star I keep in focus as I navigate life each day.

In every life story, there is a period when it seems like nothing is happening, "hibernating years," as I call them. It is like a winter season when life slows down and one seeks to find a higher purpose. Still, during the chills of a drab season in life, the warmth of love through family connectedness continues to creep its way in and blossom in our hearts.

Be it abuse, grief, past or present trauma, we owe it to ourselves, our current/future spouses, our children, and those who love us to earnestly pursue emotional healing. Because whether it happens biologically, legally, spiritually, or emotionally, motherhood—parenthood, is a gift. It is an opportunity, a responsibility to nurture and nourish—a sacred trust to secure the next generation, one which requires care and attention.

I think back on the many hibernating seasons of my life and realize that while time may not have healed my wounds as much as love did, time sure has a way of adjusting life's narratives. And boy, has the story changed since then! So, like that sunny Easter Sunday morning, when I scaled the steep entry staircase to the Philadephia Central Church, the next time someone asks you, "When will we see yours," simply smile and reply:

"Vindication is in the womb of time[86]."

SECTION 4

LIFE LESSONS

"All that is gold does not glitter,

Not all those who wander are lost;

The old that is strong does not wither,

Deep roots are not reached by the frost.

From the ashes, a fire shall be woken,

A light from the shadows shall spring;

Renewed shall be that blade that was broken,

The crownless again shall be king[87]."

J.R.R. Tolkien, Author

Chapter 9

Rivers and Rocks

"A river cuts through rock, not because of its power, but because of its persistence[88]."

James N. Watkins, Author

Washington, D.C., 2015

It was August 3rd, 2015.

It was the opening day of the weeklong Mandela Washington Fellowship Summit at the Omni Shoreham Hotel in Washington, D.C. Five hundred fellows, regally dressed in Africa's vibrant colors and costumes, found their way through security checks and into the Hall for the Summit.

The Mandela Washington Fellowship (MWF) for Young African Leaders was the flagship program of the US government's Young African Leaders Initiative (YALI) to empower young Africans through academic coursework, leadership training and networking. Once selected, fellows between the ages of 25-35 are allowed to participate in a 6-week Leadership Institute at a US university learning about Business, Civic Engagement, or Public Management.

The experience would culminate in a Summit in Washington, D.C., with inspiring American thought leaders from the public, private, and non-profit sectors. Launched initially in 2010, the MWF is a brainchild of the Obama administration and continues to serve as a US legacy project for strengthening human capital development and relations in Africa[89].

In addition to coursework, select fellows were also allowed to intern for 6 weeks at US-based non-governmental organizations, private companies, and government agencies related to their professional goals and aspirations. The institute and internship at US colleges and companies were sensational, but what every fellow most looked forward to was the coveted annual town hall with the 44th President of the United States, Barack Obama.

The opportunity to engage with the first African-American President in US history? Are you kidding? As children of the Motherland, we knew enough about the history of slavery, colonialism, the scramble for Africa, Dr. Martin Luther King, Malcolm X, and the blood-stained civil rights movement to know that what we would be witnessing was a gift. We were being offered a piece of historical pie wrapped in an unforgettable memory to last a lifetime.

Traditional outfits representing our rich ancestry were strategically chosen for the occasion. It was one thing to see the President of the United States on TV, but to have him there? Within reach? It was surreal. The session would involve some remarks delivered by President Obama, followed by a Q&A session in which he would take a few questions. Fellows prepared their questions weeks in advance for the singular moment when they would be called upon to engage the Leader of the Free World. It was a day fit for any memoir, a story worth retelling for generations to come.

Cameras clicked endlessly as everyone sought ways to immortalize the moment. We excitedly walked down the Omni Shoreham's vast corridors through the security checks and metal detectors leading into the hall. The Kenyans showed up in their colorful *enkishili*. The Ghanaians wore rich hand-woven *kente*. The Cape Verdes displayed their elaborate *panos d'obra* as the gorgeous Eswatini ladies rocked their *lihiyas*. Hundreds of fellows thronged the hall, elevating it from its original classic art deco design to a panorama of pan-African style, class, ancestry, and cultural heritage.

Grace Jerry, a disability rights activist from Nigeria, had been selected to announce the US President. When the long-awaited moment finally came, Grace wheeled onto the stage in her electric wheelchair, smartly dressed in a sterling silver lace outfit with an illustrious red and black *gele,* a nod to the ceremonial traditions of Africa's most populous economy.

President Barack Hussein Obama emerged from the shadows to a rousing, standing ovation from 500 young leaders from across the African continent. My seat directly faced the podium, giving me a bird's eye view of the unfolding scene. Here was the Commander in Chief of the most sophisticated military in the world—THE FIRST BLACK President of the United States, and at that moment, he and I were breathing the same air, occupying the same space, sharing a moment—accomplices of destiny. I had to pinch myself to be sure it was real. Tears welled up in my eyes—tears acknowledging the sacred trust to which I was privy.

His charm was no secret; his charisma knew no bounds.

President Barack Obama spoke, gliding across the stage, holding our rapt attention with his every word:

> "...our greatest challenges--whether it's inclusive development, or confronting terrorism, dealing with conflict, climate change, increasing women's rights, children's rights -- these are bigger than any one nation or even one continent. Our hope is that 10, 15, 20 years from now, when you've all gone on to be ministers in government, or leaders in business, or pioneers of social change, that you'll still be connecting with each other, that you'll still be learning from each other, and that together, you'll be reaching back and helping the next generation -- that you'll not only be making a difference in your own countries, but you'll be the foundation of a new generation of global leadership, a generation that's going to be working together across borders to make the world safer and more prosperous and more peaceful and more just. That's my hope for you[90]," he said.

Watching him then, I quickly recalled when the relatively unknown Senator Obama splashed across our screens, announcing his decision to run for President of the United States. I can still picture him, speaking daringly, on that freezing wintery day, before the Old Illinois State Capitol—at the very site where Abraham Lincoln began his own career in politics. I remembered being doubtful about his chances. Judging from Martin Luther King's assassination, if anything, I feared for his life. It's intriguing how all those fears had been replaced by the reality of the now. Barack Obama was the 44th President of the United States, and I was there—watching him with my very own eyes, hearing him without the aid of a camera or screen.

The town hall lasted a bit over an hour, an engaging Q&A

followed. Then, just when it was time to leave, President Obama stepped into the crowd and began shaking hands. In his usual warmth, he complimented fellows on their lively attires and elaborate headgears. Heading for the exit, he shook hands with as many fellows as he could; eventually, his hand slid into mine. The Secret Service did not allow selfies with the President; yet, my mind and heart took a picture that will forever remain etched in the sands of time.

On August 3, 2015, I got to meet and shake hands with President Barack Obama, and it is an experience that will stay with me for life. I had long met world leaders hanging onto the figurative tailcoat of my late Dad. This time, it was on my own merit.

That day would mean a lot to me because it was also proof of personal and professional progress against all odds. Given all the tides I had to swim against throughout my life, to build a portfolio striking enough to garner MWF selection, my handshake with POTUS 44 was a momentous milestone worth celebrating.

That is the memoir-worthy climax; let's rewind the tape a bit to how it all began, shall we? I first applied for the Mandela Washington Fellowship in 2014. Given my schedule and workload at the time, I put minimal effort into my application, hurriedly sending it off just minutes to the final deadline. My initial failure stung; still, it would serve as the impetus for me to sit up and pay a lot more attention if I wanted to succeed the next time around. The following year, I applied again. This time I was selected as part of 16 fellows representing Liberia in the 2015 cohort.

***

In my teens and into my 20s, I used to believe all it took was determination. Thankfully, the school of life was kind enough to administer a more holistic curriculum. With time, what I have discovered is that anyone can be determined. Anyone can lose a job, go looking afresh, fail at an exam, resit, pass, have a shady business deal, make losses, and start over.

Determination, in its purest form, is relatively easy. It is doable. One could even argue that it is by far the most common "common sense" solution to a snag on the road of life. Anyone can fall off a bike and, given the onlooking crowd, get back on for the shame, but it takes a different ingredient to stay on the same bike and keep peddling up a steep hill when no one is watching to encourage and applaud. It takes an extra tenacity to show up on time each day to a job in a collapsing company, to head a struggling organization, to raise a special needs child, to manage a failing economy, to maintain a trying marriage. It takes a rarer species to go to night school to get that degree in their 50s while living up to family responsibilities to children and grandchildren, to rebuild a home after multiple natural disasters, to stand by a troubled sibling, to believe in dead hopes and dreams. It takes something more elusive, something less spoken of; it takes PERSISTENCE. Anyone can sprint; let's see you do endurance running.

In global athletics, Ethiopians and Kenyans have been known to dominate long-distance running. In October 2019, Kenyan marathoner, Olympic gold medalist, and world record-holder Eliud Kipchoge became the first human in history to run a 26.2 miles marathon stretch in under 2 hours. He ran across the finish line in 1 hour, 59 minutes, and 40 seconds, defying a time limit once thought to be impossible. This is what Kipchoge had to say about his ground-breaking accomplishment:

"I'm sending a message to every individual in this world, that when you work hard, when you actually concentrate, when you set your priorities high, when you actually set your goals and put them in your heart and in your mind, you will accomplish, without any question[91]."

In the Serengeti of life, in the equation of survival of the fittest, gazelles survive the lion's hunt because, unlike their sprinting feline predators, they have been engineered as nature's best long-distance runners—ready to go the distance. Persistence is crucial in the marathon of life.

Once upon a time, in grade school, life was setting me up to be a quitter. I was becoming this girl who would admire the beauty of giving up whenever something looked hard. I would stop. Leave it to someone else to do. Sit with teary eyes behind a challenging exam paper. Get bullied and run to my brothers to rescue me. Turns out, life decided to dispossess me of all such vices of cowardice and teach me lessons in diligence, self-discipline, delayed gratification, and, yes—PERSISTENCE.

In Liberia, we have an adage that asks, *"What can water do to rock?"* The belief is that water, the "feebler" of the two, remains powerless over composite rock. The axiom suggests that "weak water" has little effect on "resolute rock." At first glance, water, depending on the flow speed, may not always dislodge a sizeable rock; still, that does not mean it has no effect. You see, water is persistent. It keeps flowing and flowing, day in and day out, summertime and winter, rainy and dry seasons, and over time, "wise water" does manage to cut through rock. Erosion and mudslides are evidence of just how much damage water can do to rocks. So to the adage, *"What can water do to rock?"* My answer? A lot. Only if water persists.

With every rock I had to push against in life, I learned very early that I would have to keep pressing harder to succeed at anything. I would have to move beyond being determined to being persistent. I had to learn, as Winston Churchill prescribes, *"to go from failure to failure without the loss of enthusiasm[92]."* My good friend Lekpele Nyamalon says: *"The world would have no inspiration if we all hid our stories of failure."*

As I look back, it is evident that my story has been enriched with chapters on failure. I have failed more than I've succeeded. I have been told "no" more times than I was ever told "yes." For each time I succeeded at anything, I first failed and had to try again two, three, four times more. Like water against rock, I had to learn to persist.

After I released my book, *"RISE! Redeeming the Future of Liberia,"* when I would give seminars at high schools and colleges across the country, people would sometimes ask me how I do it. As they put it, *"how do you manage to seamlessly move from one opportunity, job, or scholarship to the next?"* Honestly, it has never been as smooth as it looks. The failures have been many:

June 28, 2016

Good afternoon Ms. Matthews,

Thank you for applying to the 2016 - 2017 Program. We regret to inform you that you have not been selected to participate in the program this year. The 2016 recruitment cycle was one of the most competitive to date. The program received more than 5,000 applicants from 76 countries. We thank you for your dedication to sustainable development and encourage you to apply again next year.

Thank you again for your interest in our program; we wish you success in your future endeavors.

Sincerely,

Ms. XX

Senior Program Officer, Organization X

***

August 19, 2016

Dear Magdalene Ayorkor Matthews:

Thank you for your interest in the XYZ Fellowship with our organization.

Your application was carefully reviewed against the program eligibility requirements. Unfortunately, we regret to inform you that it was not selected for further consideration.

If you are interested in re-applying to the Program or exploring other employment opportunities with us, please visit our webpage.

Sincerely,

Mr. XX

Program Coordinator, XYZ Fellowship

***

May 6, 2015

Dear Magdalene Matthews,

We would like to thank you for applying for the above vacancy.

After a careful review of all candidates' backgrounds and qualifications, we regret to inform you that you have not been selected for this position.

Although you were not selected for this position, you may want to continue to review the opportunities section on our webpage.

We would like to take this opportunity to wish you continued success in the future and to thank you for your interest in our organization.

Kind regards,

Mrs. XYZ

***

One of my most unforgettable application rejections came in just seven days to my 30th birthday. Blame it on pregnancy hormones—I was expecting my son Jordan at the time, or timing. Regardless, I was deeply crushed.

March 14, 2017

Dear Mrs. Magdalene Matthews Ofori-Kuma,

On behalf of the Graduate Admissions Committee at XYZ, I thank you for your interest in our program. For the coming term, our institution was fortunate once again to receive a significant number of applications.

Given the size and strength of the applicant pool this term, the admissions process was highly competitive. After careful consideration of your application, the committee regrets that we are unable to offer you admission at this time.

We enjoyed the opportunity to learn more about your academic achievements, professional background, and commitment to public service. Again, thank you for your interest in XYZ and your continued dedication to service. We wish you success in your future endeavors as you strive to translate your personal commitment into bold social impact.

Sincerely,

XY

Director, Admissions & Financial Aid, XYZ University

***

This particular "no" really hurt. Too many no's too frequently, and there is a tendency to see it as rejection, an affirmation of our limitations, confirmation that we are not good enough. Depending on how badly we may want something, failures sting. As a result, I had to quickly unlearn determination and learn persistence. I traded in my Usain Bolt speed for Kipchoge's endurance. I had to understand early on that applying for any opportunity once just may not cut it. My Mandela Washington Fellowship application was proof of that. I also understood probability and knew that I would be increasing my chances each time I reapplied. So, as the nursery rhyme urges: I would *"try, try again."*

If my college challenges in Legon were anything to go by, it was clear from the get go that if I was ever going to get to grad school, I would have to study my head off to top my class and apply for scholarships. There was no way I could afford it otherwise. So, I studied each day like my last, sponging up complex biochemical concepts and differential equations. As far as I was concerned, every class was the main show, there was no dress rehearsal. I was determined to dot my i's, cross my t's to better position myself as an attractive candidate for any scholarship.

On top of that, I trained myself in applying for opportunities wherever I saw them. I applied for anything and everything I met the criteria for—potential job offers, scholarships, essay competitions, fellowships, etc. My strategy was simple—once I see an opportunity and I qualify, I apply. I pushed aside all the doubtful notions of, *"what if they have their own person," "what if they turn me down again,"* and submitted countless applications. When people ask what my secret is, there you have it—I apply for stuff. As you can see from the trail of rejections I've shared, I have not always been selected for everything I apply for. In fact, between 2012, after grad school, and 2013, when I landed my first management position in WASH, I applied for at least 18 jobs in Liberia; 75 percent did not work out favorably for me. But each time I failed; I would revisit the drawing board to identify areas I could strengthen. I would re-read, reformat and re-edit my resume, cover letters, and motivation statements countless times. Still, that in no way altered my resolve. Entertainment mogul Tyler Perry shares profound reflections on the notion of failure:

> *"Do you know how many times I tried to be successful at doing plays before it finally worked? From 1992 until 1998, every show I put on flopped. No one showed up, and I lost all my money. I wanted to give up. I thought I had failed, but the truth is, I never failed. Each and every time the show didn't work, I learned something new. I learned what not to do and what I could do better. You have to understand that what you may perceive to be a failure may very well be an opportunity to learn, grow, get better, and prepare for the next level. If you find the lessons in what you perceive to be failures, then you won't ever fail at anything[93]."*

With time, I have come to see "failure" and the word "no" for what they truly are—sexy, sultry, obstinate lovers; divas who know their worth and demand more wooing and cooing, wining and dining, loving and affection. I have come to see failure as an impetus to try again, a learning curve on the road to personal growth. No's hurt. Yet they are just momentary setbacks. But a "yes?" Yes, is a gamechanger. A yes could dramatically change your life with the stroke of a pen.

3 June 2011

Dear Magdalene,

Congratulations! It is with great pleasure that Professor KLM and I write to inform you that you have been selected as a Harvard Cyprus Program Scholar. This honor carries with it a financial award covering full tuition, student housing, a stipend (to be distributed in monthly payments from September 2011 through July 2012), and a coach round trip air ticket to Cyprus. If you choose to accept this award and enroll in our MS program, your tuition and student housing bills will be paid directly. In addition, we will handle your air reservations and will purchase your round-trip ticket directly.

You will receive your monthly stipend at the beginning of each month. If you intend to accept this scholarship and enroll in our MS program, please notify me no later than 10 June. If we do not hear from you by this time, we will need to offer these funds to another deserving student. Please do not hesitate to contact me if you have any questions about our program or scholarship.

Most sincerely,

Professor XYZ, Senior Lecturer on Environmental Health

What a yes that was!

My dear, take the risk and apply for stuff. Apply for that job you've always wanted, the scholarship or fellowship you've always dreamed of. Apply for any and everything you believe will drive your life and career forward. Remember, "no" changes nothing; it is merely a yellow light in the traffic of life.

Determination will get you through sprints with unbeatable world records like Usain Bolt. Still, some seasons of life, including the ongoing COVID-19 pandemic affecting us all, require endurance running à la Kipchoge.

In sum, my road to the 2015 Mandela Washington Fellowship, coupled with the culminating opportunity to meet and memorably shake hands with POTUS 44, was paved with speed-bumps. It took a lot of persistence to arrive at that single historical moment in time. Still, it was worth the ride.

Thanks to the MWF fellowship, I had the unforgettable experience of studying Public Management at the Florida International University in Miami for several weeks. I later interned with the Montgomery County Environmental Services in Dayton, Ohio, where I had the opportunity to explore and assess over a dozen water treatment plants of similar size and scope as utilities on the African continent. Thanks to the fellowship, I developed leadership and technical skills that continue to come in handy in my professional journey.

Interestingly, those three months, learning, engaging, and networking with aspiring African fellows, all leaders in their own right, on US soil, have been my most enriching immersion in pan-African excellence.

Water can cut through rock. If water persists.

IT'S A SHE

***

Chapter 10

Kintsugi

"Scars are beautiful when we see them as glorious reminders that we courageously survived[94]."

Lysa TerKeurst, Bestselling Author

In Japanese culture, the story is told of the Shogun of Japan, Ashikaga Yoshimitsu (1358-1408), who broke his favorite tea bowl and had it sent to be repaired in China. The bowl was returned with distasteful metal staples used to join the broken pieces. He ordered his craftsmen to come up with a more aesthetic solution. Legend has it that they then repaired the bowl using a lacquer dusted in powdered gold, giving rise to the philosophy and art form of "Kintsugi."

Kintsugi upholds the notion that "breaks, cracks, and repairs become a valuable and esteemed part of the history of an object, rather than something to be hidden. That, in fact, the piece is more beautiful for having been broken[95]."

Literally meaning "golden joinery" in Japanese, kintsugi is based on the belief that something broken is more durable and more beautiful because of its imperfections, the history attached to it, and its altered state. Instead of hiding what's been damaged, the shards are mended with a special resin mixed with gold dust. The bonded seams become an intrinsic part of the ceramic and add a personalized, one-of-a-kind beauty through its imperfections[96]." As bestselling author Penny Reid explains:

"The point of kintsugi is to treat broken pieces and their repair as part of the history of an object. A break is something to remember, something of value, a way to make the piece more beautiful rather than something to disguise. They use gold, not invisible superglue because mistakes shouldn't be considered ugly. Broken pieces and their repair merely contribute to the story of an object; they don't ruin it[97]."

***

Like the rest of the world, I followed in consternation as Dr. Christine Blasey-Ford appeared before the US Senate to share her experience with sexual assult during the confirmation hearings of then-Supreme Court nominee, Brett Kavanaugh. Cold and numb are the only words I can use to describe the sordid feeling that enveloped me as I watched her testimony detailing the alleged assault, which occurred 30 years before. The reactions coming in from various circles on social media, including from people I love and respect, were astonishing:

"Why did she wait this long?"

"She's just trying to ruin his career. I have a son; our sons are not protected."

"These women are all liars. What type of world do we live in when a woman can just wake up one morning and accuse an upstanding man of something he didn't do?"

My crushed soul struggled to find the courage to continue writing this manuscript, knowing fully well that I, too, ran the risk of being discounted for sharing my own experience of abuse. I went from weeks of debating, "Oh my God, what would people say," to months of, "What would people think?" I finally settled on, "Maggie, do this for you. Heal. Get the long-awaited closure that you need. Set yourself free."

Closely following the media coverage, I could not help but grieve. Grieve for this woman. Grieve for me. Grieve for every woman and girl that has had to live with the scars of abuse, the humiliation of harassment, the anguish of assault, the shackles of rape, never finding closure, never finding inner healing, never fully finding peace, desperately waiting to exhale.

I, too, am a mother to a young son, and while I empathize with the concerns raised, I am also a mother to a little girl. Beyond that, I am a woman myself—a woman who knows the sickening taste of abuse and the uphill climb it takes to claw one's broken soul out of the ditch of depression.

As the hearings proceeded, I watched as people went after her credibility and her character. What I found interesting is this: in the thousands of scenarios of women coming out, testifying of some form of abuse or the other, never had the woman been so accomplished, so above the fray, never had the woman had more to lose. The narrative has always been of an allegedly unscrupulous woman, frantically seeking her 15 minutes of fame or of the starry-eyed intern who deliberately seduces this "helpless" man in power and now wants a free ride on his renown to get ahead. There have also been tales of the gold-digging stripper pressing charges against an up-and-coming athlete after a trivial one-night stand. Still, there was never a woman involved like THIS woman.

By all standards, Dr. Ford was not your regular accuser. She was a Stanford-trained Professor of Psychology at the renowned Palo Alto University and a Research Psychologist at Stanford School of Medicine. If ever there were peaks one had to climb to be taken seriously, she had scaled them all—Ph.D. Professor. Biostatistician. Research Psychologist. Wife. Mother of two boys. She checked every high-achieving box there possibly was. Yet, when she took the bold step to share her truth, she was ridiculed; her experience, her recollection, her voice did not matter. As I soaked it all in, I now understood why I, too, had chosen the cloak of silence all these years.

So much is hidden behind a person's eyes. As she feebly read her statement before the US Congressional committee, I recognized a look in her eye that was all too familiar. One I had seen far too many times, staring in the mirror in times of helplessness. I recognized the shame, the guilt, the regret, the fear of baring your naked soul before the scornful, prying eyes of a judgmental world. But you see, silence is like a pandora's box; its power ceases to be once you yank off the lid.

For three decades—as old as I am, she lived with this secret, this sinking emotional weight upon her highly respected, intellectual shoulders. Beyond her vast publications and peer-reviewed articles, at her very core, what she revealed was a woman—a very wounded woman. By coming forward, owning her truth, she knew all too well that her world, as she had known it, would never be the same, yet she took the risk to speak up anyway. Deep down, she knew she would walk away with the one thing her professional accolades had failed to provide in 30 years of searching: closure. She would finally give herself the gift of closure.

Sometimes, I wish society would be a little more compassionate to survivors of abuse, those brave women and men who, after years of feeling so many mixed emotions, suffering in silence, finally decide to shame their shame. Outwardly, they may seem okay; they may excel even. Still, you never really know what people are dealing with in their personal lives: the silent suffering, the defeating depression, the cruel oppression, the suicidal seasons. Regrettably, society decides to humiliate them further. Their imperfections are magnified against their assailant's pristine accomplishments, with little recognition that who their perpetrator is today may be vastly different from who they were decades before when they made the rash decisions that ruined another person's life. Not every "good" person was always "good," and not every "Honorable" today has always behaved honorably. This is why empathy costs nothing. Whether you believe Dr. Ford or not, or any other person's testimony on assault, rape, racism, or harassment doesn't matter. As long as you can be empathetic enough, tolerant enough not to minimize their experience, the world just might become a little safer for us all to survive and thrive.

The #MeToo movement may have gained traction in Hollywood. But, most women the world over, by the time they hit age 20, have already had numerous experiences of someone making a move on them in an uncomfortable way. Many of these women have endured harassment, assault, rape, or were forced into child marriage. According to UN WOMEN,

> *"One in three women experience violence in their lifetime, across all social status, class, race, country or age group. For many of them, the #MeToo moment hasn't come yet, because speaking out can have fatal consequences, and survival is a long and complicated journey[98]."*

One in three women. That's my buddies, Musu, Facia, and me having lunch at our favorite grilled fish eatery in Monrovia. According to the data, one of us is likely to have experienced sexual gender-based violence in her lifetime—that one being me.

I was more than pleased to see that the 2019 theme for the UN's 16 Days of Activism[ab] Against Gender-Based Violence was Orange the World: #HearMeToo. The focus was to bring to the forefront *"the voices of women and girls who have survived violence, who are defending women's rights every day, who are taking action—many of them very far away from the limelight or media headlines."* Too many of us, across social status, class, race, country, and age groups, have suffered in silence for much too long.

Back in college, a professor once offered me a ride to my hostel as he was headed in that direction. Dad was ill and hospitalized in Ghana at the time; I was juggling classes and his care doing the two hour-long daily commute between the UG campus in Legon and the Korle Bu Teaching Hospital. I thought "Prof." was merely being supportive during a difficult time, seeing that he knew my Dad was hospitalized, and all. His later inappropriate comments on my physique were quick to unmask his true intentions. I avoided him from then on and never interacted with him outside class ever again. It was not until I got a C+ in his course at the end of the semester that I realized he had not taken my rejection too kindly.

His class was not a subject I would have gotten anything less than a B+ in. So how in the world I was graded a C+ in so simple a course remains a mystery to me. That was 14 years ago. I knew something was amiss, but I never

---

ab United Nations campaign which takes place from Nov. 25- Dec, 10 each year since 1991 to raise awareness on Gender Based Violence

reported any of it back then. On his turf, with his Ph.D., publications and laurels, it would have been the word of a female student from war-torn Liberia against that of a celebrated professor. How could I compete with that?

Some people question, why are all these women coming out now? Like me, many women know the consequences of speaking up in an environment where who you are, your gender, nationality, and even race would pale in contrast to a person of power. So, I accepted my C+ in silence and moved on, doing my best to ace the other courses, so my CGPA would not suffer.

In final year, Professor "Loverboy" was initially chosen by the Faculty research panel to serve as my Thesis Supervisor; I swiftly declined, requesting an older, more rigorous professor other students shied away from. Known to be strict in his grading, my preferred advisor had no assigned undergraduates, making the Department's response to my request quite amenable. I worked closely with Professor "Rigor" and aced my thesis based on the quality of my research.

During my defense, Professor "Loverboy," still scornful, resurfaced, attempting to punch holes in my work, questioning the integrity of the data, etc. His indignation was glaring, yet only he and I knew why. That did not stop the panel from approving a solid piece of scientific work. There would be many rumors about him and his advances. I can share this now without fear of being smeared as the desperate student who tried to seduce her helpless Professor for grades. But you see, back then, my word would not have held water against his credentials.

So, when people ask, why are all these women speaking up now?

My answer is simple: you are FINALLY listening.

Women have now risen to the pinnacles of society our grandmothers could only dream of. For the first time in over 70 years, a woman now sits at the helm of the World Trade Organization—an African woman! While there is still much ground to cover on the equality spectrum, women are now more accomplished, educated, influential, and empowered than we were a century ago. And so, we finally have your attention. And since we do, generations of us are coming forward in the quest for closure.

I recently stumbled upon an article written by a 74-year-old prominent Ghanaian BBC columnist and former Minister of State, Elizabeth Ohene. In the column, Honourable Ohene shares her own experience of sexual abuse from over 60 years before, which began when she was just seven years old. In response to her article, one of her best male friends furiously asked why she had chosen to unburden herself onto the world and *"pour out such filth into the public space,"* arguing that she could have quietly taken her unsavory 67-year-old story to her grave. Her response:

> *"Many people, mostly women, have thanked me and said it has given them the courage to deal with their own personal demons. I am humbled. If this will lead to more openness in talking about sexual practices and maybe equip and empower children to deal with abuse, I would go to my grave a happy woman[99]."*

That brings me to a crucial question: How does a person heal from sexual abuse and other forms of trauma? How does a person attain closure?

If you or someone you love has experienced physical, emotional, psychological, or sexual abuse, as challenging as it seems, there is hope. Shattered glass can be mended.

Caged birds can still sing. In the spirit of kintsugi, broken souls can be restored. The first thing I'd recommend is this: you must get professional help. At the end of the war in Liberia, there was much investment in programs targeting psycho-social counseling. The goal was to help address the deep-seated trauma of things experienced as a result of the conflict. That is because mental health is essential to physical and social well-being. We do not like to talk about this, but in the 21st century, there are uncomfortable conversations to be had in the continued quest for social equity. Award-winning author and activist L.R. Knost writes:

> "The only way to heal from the pain of the past is to walk through that pain in the present. It's terrifying, I know. It feels safer to just let the pain continue to smolder in the darkest parts of yourself. But the dark parts need tending, too, my friend."

Writing this book forced me to walk through and relive deep gut-wrenching pain in the present. It did feel safer *"to just let the pain continue to smolder in the darkest parts"* of me. It would take somber days and grim nights to find the courage to finalize some sections. But as Knost urges:

> "Don't be afraid to breathe life back into those embers of old pain, to rekindle the fires of unhealed hurts. The flames aren't there to burn you. They are there to light your way through pain to healing. You can walk through courageous and confident or shaking in your boots. It doesn't matter. Just walk through it. Hurt will transform into hope, wounds into wisdom, suffering into scars that tell of battles won and lost and of a human who survived it all."

I have survived many things in this life. Still, the journey to closure required walking through the blazing *"fires unhealed hurts."*

In Africa, the tendency to settle things "the family way," when dealing with rape and assault—especially of very young girls, without addressing the sexual trauma and mental turmoil or even punishing the perpetrator, who is perhaps a relative, has left so many, accomplished on the outside, but immensely hurting on the inside. In the few instances where the case travels beyond the secrecy of the home to the police station, they go unprosecuted due to lack of evidence. Nobel Laureate Leymah Gbowee adds her voice to condemn this pervasive culture:

> *"In 2020, there is no excuse for complacency towards sexual violence. Liberians need to stop settling rape as family matters. The government needs to harness its political will to prosecute the preparators of rape. Community members need to stop blaming, shaming, and refusing to believe rape victims when they muster the courage to speak out. This deters more women from talking about their abuse, which then invites the idea that it is perfectly fine to rape and assault women. As women, as activists, as a nation, what are we missing? How can we dismantle the rape culture[100]?"*

There can be no cookie-cutter, "family way" solution to sexual abuse. Some people were abused by their own parents and guardians while very little; others by relatives or family friends as they grew older. Additionally, some were abused by authority figures they would have never imagined could have harmed them in such a cruel way. Some reported it and were dismissed. Like me, others never told a soul, living with the guilt and shame for decades to come. Everyone's experience of and reaction to abuse are unique. There is no blueprint for abuse and the level of damage caused to a person's mental, physical, and emotional health, so there can be no quick-fix, one-size-fits-all solution to how people heal from such a terrible wrong.

In some cases, it may be an instant spiritual experience; in others, it may take years of psycho-social counseling, deep soul-searching, journaling, meditation, and daily affirmations. For someone else, it may mean finding the courage to speak up, to tell your story, to own your pain, to forcefully yank the bandage of silence off, and finally let the wound heal in the open air. It may require finding your tribe, joining a support group, people of kindred spirits, and similar experiences to understand and support your recovery process. It may require reading relevant books on healing from sexual and emotional abuse and applying those methods into your daily experience. Whatever the case may be, no one else can determine the healing process for you, or define how structured and how pretty it should look, simply because no one else lived through that horrendous experience with you. It was your cross to bear and your bullet to bite. How you recover from it depends entirely on how your shattered soul sees fit to be mended. Still, one thing is paramount, whatever it will take for you to heal, get closure, finally move on, and live free from the shackles of despair, make sure you do that.

Preacher and author Joyce Meyer, in her revealing memoir, *Beauty for Ashes*, which I found to be the most persuasive manual I came across on my own journey to closure, warns:

"There are two kinds of pain: the pain of change and the pain of never changing and remaining the same."

She suffered years of abuse at the hands of her own father and writes to motivate others to heal. To the hurting people reading this, know this, hurting people hurt people. It is high time to stop bleeding on the people who did not cut you. Life coach Iyanla Vanzant cautions:

> *"Until you heal the wounds of your past, you are going to bleed. You can bandage the bleeding with food, with alcohol, with drugs, with work, with cigarettes, with sex; but eventually, it will all ooze through and stain your life. You must find the strength to open the wounds, stick your hands inside, pull out the core of the pain that is holding you in your past, the memories, and make peace with them[101]."*

Many of us have hidden decades of pain beneath layers of degrees, awards, eyeshadow, concealers, Gucci, Louis Vuitton, drugs, and alcohol. We swept it under the carpet long enough. Now it's time to heal. Address that hurt. Get serious help. Refuse to raise children, manage life, or lead others with the shackles of a wounded soul. Heal.

I am no expert on mental health and trauma recovery. Everything I share or refer to here is based on lived experience, coupled with research findings I came across while processing my own healing. When embarking on a similar restorative journey from sexual trauma, remember:

> *"Recovering from sexual assault takes time, and the healing process can be painful. But you can regain your sense of control, rebuild your self-worth, and learn to heal[102]."*

Experts Vanessa Marin and Dr. Laura McGuire recommend the following recovery strategies[103]:

1. *Feel all your feelings without shame.*

2. *If one of your feelings is that what happened was your fault, try to replace that with compassion for yourself.*

3. *Seek professional help as soon as you feel up to it.*

4. *If you have a partner, consider going to therapy together; your partner should consider going individually, as well.*

5. *Call on family and friends — but choose your sources of support carefully.*

6. *Listen to your own thoughts.*

7. *Read a book that helps you get to know your body again.*

8. *Make a list of your triggers.*

9. *Don't try to ignore your feelings if you're triggered.*

10. *Make a "safe" list too.*

11. *You deserve pleasure. Pursue it.*

12. *Practice saying "no."*

13. *Do all the things that make you feel happy and at peace.*

14. *Celebrate good sexual experiences.*

15. *Remember that while you may face triggers for the rest of your life, this doesn't mean you're broken.*

In addition to seeking professional help, another thing I found incredibly liberating was writing. In *The Courage to Heal*, another excellent resource for your library, Ellen Bass and Laura Davis counsel:

> *"Writing is an important avenue for healing because it gives you the opportunity to define your own reality. You can say: This did happen to me. It was that bad. It was the fault and responsibility of _____. I was—and am—innocent."*

Writing was vital to my healing process, allowing me to own my narrative. It compelled me to find my voice and my roar!

Locked in the message of kintsugi is the fact that immense strength and inherent beauty lie in your brokenness. Own it. Like T.D. Jakes admonishes:

> *"I found out that the things that hurt us the most can become the fuel and the catalyst that propel us toward our destiny[104]."*

Stop waiting for permission; go ahead and exhale! Learn as much as you can if that is what you want. Write that book if you have the passion. Buy that car if you can afford it; build that house of your dreams. Life should not stop because you are single, a woman, uneducated, a mother, or on a journey to emotional healing. It should rather elevate. Be it romantically or socially, anyone who genuinely loves and deserves you will never be intimidated by the full package of you.

As bleak as it seems, beyond the brokenness, wholeness is possible. Mend your scars with the gold lacquer of hope, knowing that:

> *"Without those times of turmoil and change, the ups and downs, we would not be able to learn and grow or enrich our lives. The struggles will become your story, and that's the beauty of kintsugi. Your cracks can become the most beautiful part of you[105]."*

Make an intentional, conscientious decision that you will not finish reading this book without making a firm resolve to embark on the path to inner healing. Hold your feet to the fire to begin applying the recovery strategies in this chapter. The journey of a thousand miles begins with that first step: a decision to leave where you are to become the best version of you, you could possibly be. As inspirational author Shannon L. Adler cautions:

"Forget what hurt you in the past, but never forget what it taught you[106]."

Take charge of your life. In the words of motivator Steve Maraboli:

"The truth is unless you let go, unless you forgive yourself, unless you forgive the situation, unless you realize that the situation is over, you cannot move forward.[107]"

Make a vow to yourself that no matter what, you will live your life to the full.

"A caged bird stands on the grave of dreams,

his shadow shouts on a nightmare scream

his wings are clipped, and his feet are tied..."

But guess what?

He still *"opens his throat to sing[108]."*

IT'S A SHE

***

212

Chapter 11

Dare

"You can never leave footprints that last if you are always walking on tiptoe[109]."

Leymah Gbowee, Nobel Laureate

Nairobi, 2018

It was one of those exhausting Saturday nights. There I was, sprawled lazily on the carpet trying to put my son to sleep. I had moved to Nairobi at the beginning of the year to take on an international assignment and was gradually finding my rhythm. That Saturday, like many others, I kicked off the day running errands. First, there was a quick stop at the salon to get my hair done, then another by the market for food supplies. I rushed back home and wrapped up the day, cooking several sauces and stews to cover for lunch and dinner for the coming work week.

By evening, I was visibly fatigued. The single item left on my to-do list was to tuck Jordan to bed. Lying snuggly next to him, I patted his back and watched as he slowly dozed off, his breathing becoming deeper as sleep crept in. The TV played on in the shadows, providing the only background light to this precious mother-child moment. I slowly stand, ready to take him into his bed, when the image across the screen caught my eye...

"This is for her,

The woman whose voice could not be dimmed as it rose from the dark,

Who fueled hope for those who had it once put out,

The woman who never learned to read but made sure her daughter graduated,

Who wanted the title of mother, but also that of CEO.

This is for her,

The woman who held her head high, and her placard even higher,

Who tirelessly spent her days at work and her nights helping with homework,

Who knew her payslip should reflect her worth and not her gender.

This is for her,

The woman who drives change in a world many consider to be driven by men.

For all the women who light the way,

We dedicate the new Hyundai Creta."

I stopped in my tracks, nestling my son in both arms while soaking in what I had just seen. Those 60 seconds left me feeling more empowered as a woman, more seen as a person, more... understood.

"Light the Way" was a 1-minute advert for Hyundai conceptualized by the brand's team in South Africa, but in the stillness of the night, it was more than just an ad

for a sleek car. It was a message. An ideal. An aspiration. In 60 seconds, they left me dead curious about a car I could not afford and utterly infused with a sense of pride in the remarkable mosaic that is womanhood. As I added finishing touches to this manuscript while pregnant with my precious daughter, Mishan, I, too, have come to realize, indeed, "this is for her."

As a woman, a wife, a mother, and a professional, it took a lot of courage and recollection to pen these thoughts so vulnerably on paper and share my story so intimately. I battled long-standing reservations on whether to raise my voice and bare my soul. I wrote much of this book carrying life in my womb, while performing figurative triple bypass surgeries on my heart.

So much past had to be revisited, so many memories reawakened, so much pain relived. I had to distance myself from the mundane to allow my soul a winter of renewal on the journey to closure. My daughter's kicks as I typed the night away would be the reminder whisking me back to reality, re-echoing the words, "This is for her."

Whenever I would toy with the idea of giving up, abandoning this project midway, I'd recall that lazy Saturday night, in my dimly-lit living room, when a car commercial would inspire me to continually aspire to be a woman who lights the way.

***

History is rife with tales of disruption.

From the legends of Alexander the Great's conquests, the erection of the pyramids in Egypt, to Yaa Asantewa's uprising to defend the Ashanti cultural heritage—history depends on disruptors. Modern-day Ghana is home to one of the few surviving Kingdoms in Africa, the Ashanti Kingdom—all thanks to Yaa Asantewa's courage.

Meanwhile, one of the classic children's books we are made to read growing up is a tale centered on staying in one's place—Charles Dickens' *The Adventures of Oliver Twist*. A piece of literature instilling in us early the societal expectation of not asking for more like naughty little Oliver did. Lofty dreams are surgically removed under the scalpel of a single story, leaving us only desirous to be good, contented little children.

Society goes a step further to reinforce this message when introducing us to the arts—teaching us how to color, yet, only to color in the lines. They expose us to crayons, pastels, and water paint, all that fun stuff, with one caveat:

"Be creative, be expressive but make sure you stay within the lines."

So we grow up, living carefully, not realizing that we were coded from childhood not to question the status quo. With our creative genius stifled and our abstract expressions muffled, we are left incapable of ambition, terrified of disruption, and completely cautious to never color outside the lines. But what would happen if we did?

What would the world look like?

What would we look like?

Who would you be if you were completely free of the expectations of society?

Which version of you would the world see?

What would happen if we stopped conforming?

What would you achieve if only you'd dare?

This is one life lesson I learned the hard way...

***

"To get ahead, you have to be humble in this life."

"Maggie, don't show yourself too much."

"It's distasteful to draw attention to yourself and your accomplishments."

"You always have to let other people praise you."

Those were my skewed philosophies and narrow mindset from years of listening to people's advice as I geared up to serve as a panelist at a women's speaking event at the historic American University in Washington, D.C., in August 2015.

It was very early fall in the US capital, and the weather was rather lovely, still warm and sunny. I had picked out a pink African Ankara outfit just for the event, in keeping with the season. I took extra care to dab finishing touches to my faint makeup as I went over my remarks in my head for the umpteenth time. This would be my first international speaking engagement in which I was invited as an author and not a water specialist. I was clearly excited and nervous at the same time.

Over the years, I had attended meetings in my technical capacity to discuss the water and sanitation issues in Africa, developing much confidence along the way. This time around, as the invitation instructed, I would have to come across as a *"woman Power Player contributing to the growth and transformation of the people and the environment around them, both on the African continent and in the diaspora."* I sighed at the thought of what all that meant. I read the profiles of my co-panelists and felt even more intimidated: "What am I even going to say?" I pondered.

The event started at 4:30 pm on the dot. I had gotten there nearly an hour too early, so I treated myself to a mini-tour of the beautiful AU campus. My childhood buddy Joemade Scott, who lived in the Maryland area, was kind enough to show up with much-needed moral support. Ever the life of the party, Joemade brought along lots of humor and was super thrilled to hear me speak. I had even taken along a few copies of my book *RISE: Redeeming the Future of Liberia*, if the occasion allowed me to showcase my book.

The session kicked off to a fantastic start; my bio, along with that of my three co-panelists, was read. We were then politely ushered to a high table to share reflections on the topic: *Africa 3.0: How Women Leaders Are Shaping the Continent and Improving the Continent's Development Prospects*. The discussion was rich, the panelists knowledgeable, and the audience engaging. When it was my turn to speak, I remembered all the voices reminding me not to draw attention to myself. I talked about Africa in generic terms, casting the lens so far away from my personal reflections and achievements. I made no mention of my book, which was on the stand right outside the auditorium door. Weighing in on all those voices, I refused to blow my own horn. I stayed "humble," played it safe, and after a few brief sentences, was done speaking.

"They will eventually see it on their way out," I thought.

The audience appreciated my comments and inputs, and judging from Joemade's recording of the session, I realized that I had forwarded some useful insights. Still, I had not projected myself in the totality of who I was and my actual contribution to "shaping the continent" and helping improve "the continent's development prospects" through self-empowerment, youth development, and nation-building. I made no reference to the self-funded seminars I had conducted for Voinjama and Nimba County Community Colleges or the pep rallies at the Salvation Army and J.J. Roberts United Methodist Schools in Monrovia. I said nothing of the book donations I had made to deserving students and school libraries at multiple public and private high schools and colleges across Liberia. Again, I was extra careful to not "show myself too much." I colored inside the lines. I conformed.

Minutes later, the next panel discussion kicked off. Out came these two dynamic Nigerian sisters, both panelists, who would quickly teach me a lesson I would never forget. They had both grown up in the States and were actively engaged with diverse projects individually but had paired up to write a book entitled, *"Whose Shoes Are You Wearing?"* When it was their turn to speak, they cut to the chase and went for gold. They drove their generic point home and quickly moved on to pitch their book and why it's a must-read and IS AVAILABLE for purchase on the stand outside.

At the close of their session, participants queued outside to purchase their book and take selfies with the authors. The queue rapidly grew longer; the sisters brought out even more copies from a nearby purple carry-on, tucked away discreetly under the table. It was clear to me then that these ladies had not come to play. With just a few words, these remarkable Nigerian sisters managed to turn an African women's speaking engagement to which they were invited into their personalized book-signing event, autographing messages to each customer. Soon they needed an extra table to move things along. Since no one was flocking to my bookstand, my books were quickly relegated to the registration table, near the pile of name tags, markers, and stationery. My book, the precious investment of my time and intellect, found its place in the shadows of oblivion as these two driven African women unapologetically took center stage.

So impressed was I with their pitch, thoughts, and presentation that I, too, queued up to buy a copy, gather autographs, and pose with the authors.

And so, ladies and gentlemen, that is how I took all my books back home. THE END.

Let's assess my predicament a bit, shall we? As authors, could we not have all co-existed in the sandbox of the moment, jointly sharing our gifts with the world? We most definitely could have. But you see, I did not allow it. Heeding the limiting voices of "be humble, don't talk too much about yourself" is how I regrettably took every single copy of my book back home. I lost a perfect opportunity to get my book out to a broader international audience because I was "humble." So many of us live in prisons in our minds, wills, and emotions, struggling to break free from societal expectations of our age, race, gender, or nationality. Roy T. Bennett, in *The Light in the Heart,* puts it like this:

> *"The biggest wall you have to climb is the one you build in your mind: Never let your mind talk you out of your dreams, trick you into giving up. Never let your mind become the greatest obstacle to success. Get your mind on the right track, the rest will follow[110]."*

My mentor once said to me, life's growth and changes hinge on answering one critical question: *Can you grow into this role?* To paraphrase, can you dare? Whether it's the role of manager, wife, mother, or matron—a newer version of you, a daringly disruptive you, will be required to step up to the responsibilities of that role. Can you muddy the waters, think outside the box, or throw away the entire box, if need be? Can you stretch the limits of your potential to want more, dream more, and be more? Can you, just for a moment, forget what you were taught from Oliver's tale and allow yourself to dream lofty dreams like Cinderella? If we're going to base our lives on children's classics, why not choose stories that push us to dare like Mulan and make history like Pocahontas?

I learned many things that day from those "Naija girls." Life was kind enough to offer us the same platform, in the same place, on the same day. Yet, we went away with different outcomes. They were willing to put themselves out there. I was still seeking society's permission to do so. I realized after much dismay, as we say in Liberia, "if you do not say I am, another will never say "thou art." And so, I have made a conscious decision to dare ever since.

This book is a reflection of that dare. On the professional front, likewise. After a half-decade of diligent development work, actively contributing to rebuilding post-conflict Liberia's water sector, I took a dare. I decided it was time to broaden my professional horizons by actively pursuing opportunities across the global WASH sector. I stopped shying away from who I was, seeking validation, and gave myself permission to be. I stopped asking questions like: "what would people think" and started asking myself, "can I grow into this role?"

Am I willing to invest time to learn, grow, upgrade, study, read, burn the midnight candle, conceive, write and pursue the vision? If my answer is yes, I go after it. In the words of Shakespeare:

> *"Cowards die many times before their deaths; The valiant never taste of death but once[111]."*

I already know what happens when I accept the status quo, when I don't dare—when I don't at least try. I already know what happens when I silently conform. At this point in my life and career, I am curious to see what happens when I don't. Author Vironika Tugaleva sums up my thoughts perfectly:

"You are not who you think you are.

You are not your fears, your thoughts, or your body.

You are not your insecurities, your career, or your memories.

You're not what you're criticized for, and you're not what you're praised for.

You are a boundless wealth of potential. You are everything that's ever been.

Don't sell yourself short.

Every sunset, every mountain, every river, every passionate crowd, every concert, every drop of rain - that's you.

So, go find yourself.

Go find your strength, find your beauty, find your purpose.

Stop crafting your mask. Stop hiding.

Stop lying to yourself and letting people lie to you.

You're not lacking in anything except awareness.

Everything you've ever wanted is already there, awaiting your attention, awaiting your time[112]."

All you have to do is dare.

On a warm evening in Washington D.C., those impressive Nigerian-American sisters would be my wake-up call to dare—one I have never forgotten since.

Chapter 12

Living Free

"Freeing yourself was one thing; claiming ownership of that freed self was another[113]."

Toni Morrison, American Literary Great

In this final chapter, I wish to tell you a story...

A true story, set in the Nakuru highlands of colonial Kenya...

Once upon a time, there lived a man named Lord Maurice Egerton. In the former British Kenya colony, he was the 4th Baron of Egerton and sole heir of noble parents Alan de Tatton and Lady Anna Louisa Taylor. Lord Egerton found himself in love with a Lady believed to be a distant relation to Queen Elizabeth. To win her heart, the English nobleman built an imposing castle in the area known in colonial times as East Africa's White Highlands to impress the lady he so desperately wanted to marry.

Lord Egerton hired one of the best architects in England and brought in 100 Indians for the construction work. He imported green marble from Italy, oak from England, and tiles from China to build this colossal 4 story, 52 room architectural wonder on his massive 22,000-acre property.

It would take all of 16 years to construct, from 1938 all the way to 1954. But guess what?

In the end, his beloved lady turned him down. She never cared to visit the continent, not even once, to see the luxurious home he had so lovingly built for her. She went on to marry another British noble who made his home and mansion in Australia instead.

Let us just say the heart wants what it wants. Heartbroken, from then until Lord Maurice Egerton died in 1958, he resigned to a life of solitude. Then in a vindictive move, he shockingly banned all females from stepping on his property ever again. No woman was ever allowed to visit the castle or the grounds, and Lord Egerton never proposed to another woman in his lifetime. Four years later, he died, unwedded and childless, making him the 4th and final Baron of Egerton. Today, his lavish home, the Egerton Castle, stands cold, unoccupied, 14 km outside Nakuru City, Kenya's 4th largest urban enclave—a testament of just how far a man would go for love and just how low he'd descend under the weight of a broken heart.

Dubbed the *"castle of love and hate,"*[114] I was privileged to visit Lord Egerton's Castle in 2018. While many would describe the Baron's tale as a 20th century Shakespearean tragedy, walking through the gloomy halls, I realized it was also a proverb on life. It was an ironic lesson to LIVE.

The Baron was noble and wealthy, he could have married any other damsel of his choosing, in Kenya, Britain, Australia, India, or otherwise, but he chose not to. There were many options available to him. He could have chosen a marriage of convenience in the hopes that love would follow. Yet, he would not take a second shot at love. By failing to grow beyond a single life's disappointment, he denied his possible progeny the chance of ever seeing the light of day.

The lush castle grounds would never feel the bustling feet of bashful children.

The cold walls would never know the warmth of a woman.

The dark halls would never feel the awakening caress of gentle laughter.

His noble lineage would sadly end with him.

He died the 4th and final Baron of Egerton.

What a tragedy! His story is a stark reminder that wealth does not always gurarantee a productive life.

What exactly have I learned these past 30 years around the sun? I have learned to live. I have learned to take multiple heart-wrenching disappointments and ride them like a surfboard on the waves of life into destiny. I learned to plunge into the deep, stepping away from the safe shores. I have observed that only those who go down to the sea in ships, brave enough to do business in deep waters, get to see wonders in the deep[115]. There is so much more to the earth than dry land, but you would never know if all you did was stay close to shore.

For all his wealth and nobility, the broken-hearted Lord Egerton was unable to appreciate that. So instead of seeing what else life had to offer in the vast expanse of the British Empire, he resigned to a life of seclusion and regret. Author Anne Lamott captures this sentiment powerfully:

> *"What if you wake up someday, and you're 65, or 75, and you never got your memoir or novel written; or you didn't go swimming in warm pools and oceans all those years because your thighs were jiggly and you had a nice big comfortable tummy; or you were just*

so strung out on perfectionism and people-pleasing that you forgot to have a big juicy creative life, of imagination and radical silliness and staring off into space like when you were a kid? It's going to break your heart. Don't let this happen[116]."

When I look over my life, it is clear that the woman I am today was forged in the fires of vicissitudes—childhood abuse, the passing of my Dad and brother, uphill climbs through school, marriage, and motherhood. I have had countless other challenges—health scares, miscarriage, loss of some very near and dear friends and family, betrayal, disappointments. Still, somehow after every roadblock, something in me has kept going. It seems these collective experiences birthed a certain resilience, a persistence that has kept me going from one challenge to the next, ever hopeful.

My first decade of life taught me: "Never lose sight of your brother." Given their activism at the time, our parents believed if ever we were to be in danger, we would have a greater chance of making it out alive if we stuck together. I still make it a point to regularly keep in touch with my brothers across distance and time. We still need each other to get through life.

My second decade of life was one of surviving and thriving through loss. I learned that the story doesn't always go according to plan. Still, you never, ever give up. You wake up every day, and you show up. You give it your best and trust that things will all work out just fine. I learned this by watching my parents pick life back up every time Liberia's recurring conflict would take our family back to square one.

In recent years, my favorite movies are biopics and documentaries based on true-life stories. I am all for an action-packed Marvel classic on a Friday night to unwind after a busy week. Still, I would rather watch an adaptation of someone's life any day. What I find most fascinating is not just who they have become now, but the starting point, the journey, the process, the ups and downs, the broken road that led them to today. I like to see the tears and laughter, be invited in to share their joys and sorrows. I want to know what went into the making of the man or woman.

I admire their Grammy awards and dance to the songs, but what I'm most intrigued by is what it took to transform googly-eyed teenage girls from shy Misses into the powerhouse gospel sensation, The Clark Sisters. I want to know how Simone Biles coped with life with an addicted Mom and her adoption by her grandparents. I want to feel her heartache soldiering on through years of practice to become the greatest gymnast of all time, with signature moves in her name. I want to get a glimpse into a person's "why" and their "how." Don't just show me the prim and proper, gold and glitter; let me in on the messy, self-doubt, and second-guessing. I know their accomplishments; I can easily google that, and the internet will have so much to say. What I'm interested in is their frailty, their humanity, that thing that I could relate to and hold onto in my own race towards the sun.

If asked to describe my life so far, in a sentence, I would say my life has been a remarkable mix of authentic Liberian jollof rice. While our Nigerian and Ghanaian cousins continue to debate on whose version of the West African delicacy is best, once you've tried, you'll agree, like my husband, Dennis, that Liberia's take on the dish takes the trophy any day. In sum, my journey has been a sour-sweet panorama of ingredients, tucked into tomato sauce and allowed to simmer over time.

In the shadows of war, suspense, drama, abuse, disappointments, death, and tragedy, there have been notable victories, beautiful memories, healthy babies, and a supportive family. There have been "the bad" and "the ugly," yet there have also been "the melodious and memorable." In the soil of insecurities have blossomed the seeds of self-confidence, self-discipline, and self-worth.

As I reflect on this remarkable journey of restoration, I realize there have been three core elements holding everything in place, weaving their way through the tapestry of my life:

- Faith, Family, and Fortitude.

My Christian faith has been critical in defining my values and moral compass. Reflecting on the years, I see that my belief in God has kept me anchored through changing seasons and times and taken me through many tragedies. I would recite the *23rd Psalm* and Longfellow's *A Psalm of Life* endlessly as a source of comfort throughout my Dad's week-long funeral events and the long mourning season after that. My faith has played a significant role in keeping me sane, keeping me doing, keeping me loving, and keeping me striving. I remain a firm believer in the power of God to take a messy situation and bring out a message that would later minister hope, comfort, and direction. As prelate Jackie McCullough puts it,

> *"There is no waste in the economy of God. That means that there is nothing that has happened to you that God will not use to accomplish His will[117]!"*

So, I remain hopeful that a beautiful butterfly will emerge out of the caterpillar I used to be.

Then there have been my family and friends. Psychologist

Paul Bloom says, *"Humans are social beings, and we are happier, and better when connected to others[118]."* My tribe has supported me through the countless tests, trials, and triumphs of life. In Africa, we say, *"It takes a village to raise a child."* It took a village, literally, to help make me the woman I am today. Many people left positive influences on me and etched indelible footprints in the sands of my heart.

Some of my fondest memories stem back to Abidjan, to Allyson Browne. I smile at the thought of her. How to describe such an iconic woman? I'll borrow the words of author Nikki Rowe:

> *"She entered the room, and the entire crowd stopped; who was she? Even in a million moons, you will never understand her, for she is too mysterious to presume and too wise to share her light with everyone. I wanted to love her, but I could tell I wasn't the only one[119]."*

Allyson Browne was the first complete picture of the woman I wanted to be when I grew up. She was a mother, a professional, a sister, a friend, and a mentor. I would first meet her at church. She would show up on Sundays, elegantly dressed, in tastefully tailored batik, matching accessories, and a disarming smile. She was gorgeous and exuded a world of confidence. Her young son, Jordan—an older namesake of mine, would always be at her side. I admired her.

Aunty Allyson took me into her heart and life, showing me the ropes to corporate life. She would take me to her office in *Plateau*, Abidjan's commercial district, where I would watch her work, strategize for the future, chair meetings, and deliver results. She would close for the day and head home and put just as much finesse into caring for her son.

Aunty Allyson had an endearing relationship with her Mom, which was so charming to see. She was the first person that pushed me to learn to type, allowing me hours of practice on her office and home computers—a skillset I am grateful for as I type this.

I remember trying my hands at my first prose during those many days in her office, excited to share them with her each time. Long before I knew I loved writing or was even gifted at it, she encouraged me. As far as role models go, as a teenage girl with lofty dreams, Allyson Browne was it for me. It didn't matter what she did, wore, or said; she did it all with class. Bold, beautiful, brilliant, and gracious, I had no idea what it would take to be all those things, but she set a standard I was inspired to meet someday.

Of course, there was my foster sister Kate. Kate was Mom's buddy, Albertha Clarke's daughter, but as far as we were concerned, she was as good as Mom's. Her family lived across the street from ours on 10th Street, Sinkor, but Kate lived at our house. The only girl for my parents, Kate Clarke, turned out to be the sophisticated big sister every girl dreamt of. With my first and most enduring playmate being my brother Martin from birth straight up until elementary, Kate and the other female foster siblings who lived with us were my baptism into femininity. She made sure my hair was always neat. She would have it done regularly at her Mom's nearby *Taylor and Clarke Beauty Salon*, relaxing and conditioning it when necessary, finishing it off with large, bouncy, Shirley Temple curls that I got to wear to church on Sundays. Boy! Would I show up feeling like an adorable Princess in Sunday School at St. Stephen's Church!

Kate was a good six years older than me and was the perfect combination of beauty, brains, and athleticism. She had gorgeous, dark-chocolate skin filled with rich, glowing melanin with the heartiest smile. She brought in good grades and even represented Liberia on the national track team, competing internationally at the 1996 Summer Olympics. When Kate flew out to Sweden in 1995 for the World Athletics Championships, that was it. She provided me with my first image of a high-achieving, goal-oriented, self-motivated young lady out to make her mark in the world.

Another positive influence was Mrs. Catherine Swen, my 3rd-grade teacher at J.J. Roberts School in Liberia. In her class, I landed a double promotion from 3rd grade to 5th, propelling me to ultimately graduate from high school at age 16. With my grades consistently hitting the Principal's Special list, she recognized my skills and pushed me early to succeed. We sometimes take this for granted, but for a child, it's life-changing to have a teacher who can spot talent and train it. Mrs. Swen is my first recollection of a teacher that identified and pruned my potential. Her positivity equipped me to face many challenges to come.

Then there was the Clarke family. Romeo and Nomor Clarke would come to be the Godparents every young woman wishes she had. Their children Romeo Jr., Lionel, and Roundelle, had been my schoolmates back in elementary school. Years later, Nomor Clarke's and my path would cross again during another one of my stints with the UN. With her wealth of experience, foresight, and motherly demeanor, our relationship naturally grew from there. With my closest family away, their house became home, and I have gladly been a 4th Clarke sibling ever since.

Another key influence on my life has been my church family. From Monrovia to Abidjan, Accra, Port Harcourt, Nairobi, and the US, I have been blessed to meet and interact with an incredible larger church family that would help shape my understanding of various aspects of life including singlehood, parenting, and marriage. Christian values would come to play a significant role in my decision-making, providing a moral compass through tricky stages of life.

At church, I was blessed to be surrounded by many amazing people who believed in and encouraged me. I learned that every person needs to have a *Paul*, a *Silas*, and a *Timothy* to get by in life. Figuratively, Paul is your mentor, a knowledgeable, experienced guide, someone you look up to for wisdom and counsel as you sail through life. Silas is a friend at your level with whom you share your successes and failures, laughter, and tears. Someone with whom you can relate, be real, expose your vulnerabilities, and be your authentic self without judgment. Then there's Timothy. Timothy is your mentee, someone of the next generation that you are consciously pouring into. Someone you are mentoring and encouraging to grow into the best version of themselves that they can be.

I have kept this *Paul—Silas—Timothy* wisdom close when managing relationships in my life. I have come to learn that it is easy to find "Silas." In fact, depending on how well things are going in your life at a given time, you may find yourself surrounded by many self-proclaimed Silases and Timothy's—people who associate with you or desire to be mentored by you because of your social status and accomplishments. However, I have learned that if you will go far in life, survive the stormy rains and waist-deep snows, emotional highs, and mental lows, it is crucial to stay in tune with your Paul. Wisdom and experience matter. One piece of advice from Paul could spare you a lifetime of shipwrecks. Just be sure to weigh his/her motives to ascertain that Paul is in your best interest. I have been fortunate to be surrounded by many people playing their part as Paul, Silas, and Timothy, through the changing scenes of life. They have each contributed in meaningful ways to making me the person I am today. I have had my very own orchestra of people praying, counseling, mentoring, funding, and inspiring me along life's road.

Staying focused has not always been easy, especially in the modern-day world, with so much screaming for your attention. My tribe has helped me keep my eyes on the prize. An introvert by nature, I have had many friends, yet few very close ones. Lloa and I bonded when we were in diapers. Then there were Jerlyn, Estelle, and Mariama in high school in Abidjan. Rachael stepped into my world when I moved back to Liberia in 2003, and we quickly jived. Beatrice was my big-sister friend, advising me on life's decisions. Sylvia and I connected in college. From 2nd year of college until we graduated, she made sure I had all the notes, information, and moral support I needed to graduate even though I was dealing with so much in school. Her passing as this manuscript went to print was a significant blow for me.

Musu walked into my life during a season of great uncertainty when life presented more questions than answers. We were churchmates that evolved into best friends. Musu's warmth, care, and love for babies would make her my go-to person whenever I had an issue with the kids. Her prayers, love, and support proved valuable as I processed the mosaic of emotions on this journey to closure. My "ride and conquer," as I call her, she's the Gail to my Oprah, the Silas to my Paul. Musu, whom we've tenderly nicknamed "Fairy" for her role as Fairy Godmother to everyone, remains an immense pillar of love and friendship, which I'm ever grateful to have in my corner.

Then there is Nina. Ah! My Nina! Nina is one of Bishop

George and Reverend Musu Harris' four amazing daughters who would become my sisters. As one of my favorite little sisters and younger best friends, her unwavering love for me helped anchor me through many storms. It was Anais Nin that said:

"Each friend represents a world in us, a world possibly not born until they arrive, and it is only by this meeting that a new world is born[120]."

Like I said, faith, family, and lastly, fortitude. Merriam-Webster defines *"fortitude"* as the *"strength of mind that enables a person to encounter danger or bear pain or adversity with courage[121]."* It denotes strength of character and two of my favorite words, resilience, and persistence. Fortitude denotes the analogy of water finding its way around rocks. Fortitude is the process whereby we evolve from mere determination, a first step, to the place of endurance. It is that place where you embrace the wisdom of long-suffering. Fortitude is essential on the journey. Looking back at my life, I hear fortitude screaming at critical junctures, spurring me on.

***

As I bring this manuscript to a close, several acknowledgments come to mind.

If I could write a letter to the older generation...

To the remarkable men and women that went ahead of me, I would thank them for their vulnerability. I would thank them for allowing me a peek into their humanity. I would thank them for the many ways they exposed their nakedness to teach me how to clothe my own. I would thank them for their patience and candor in sharing precious wisdom. As the African proverb goes: "What an old man sees while sitting down, a child cannot see even if he climbs up a tree." Lastly, I would humbly ask that they continue to carefully protect their sharp minds and waning bodies to lengthen the opportunities we have to benefit from the wealth of their foresight.

If I could write a letter to my late Dad, I would say,

"Dad,

I am honored to have been your child. For the "good genes and sharp head," as you used to say, the immense compassion for others, the passionate pursuit of excellence, and the unflinching resilience you exemplified and passed onto us all, I am most grateful! As your only Princess, I miss you deeply each day. The silent flame of inner strength lit all so early in my subconscious has stayed emblazoned deep within me during the most challenging times of my life. I could never share the many milestone moments of my life with you, but each day I look in the mirror, every time I hold a pen in my left hand, with each nascent idea I come up with, I see tangible proof that you were here. Your DNA whispers through me. Thank you for laying the bedrock on which I stand. Rest in power."

If I could write a letter to my Mom, I would tell her I love her:

"Dear Mama,

I love you. I always have and always will. I want you to know that I see you, I see YOU. I see your efforts; I see your strength. I admire how through everything life has thrown your way—a challenging childhood, political prison, deferred dreams, love, and loss, you have survived. You manage to smile so wide; it warms the coldest heart.

Thank you, sweet mother, for giving so much of yourself for me. I plan to give you your flowers as much as I can; however, I can. Nothing has ever been too precious to share with me. Thank you for always believing in the beauty of my dreams and encouraging me to keep trying. If I can, but just gladden your heart, make you proud, I will know that I have tried, in my imperfection, to let you know how much I appreciate your perfect love."

To my siblings,

Fellas, I promise that I will keep on striving. The blood in our veins is one of passion, it is one of promise, and it is one of purpose. We owe it to the legacy we stand on to pursue our deep-seated passions, live up to our convictions, and fulfill our God-given purpose. No matter the challenge, no matter the uphill climb, I will endeavor to remind myself that I "have been assigned this mountain" to show others, it can be moved[122].

To my loving husband Dennis,

My beloved Etonam, one book will never do. Thank you for being the wind beneath my wings and anchor through the storm. Thank you for standing with me and encouraging me in this pursuit of emotional healing and inner peace. I promise to stay true, prayerful, and purposeful on this journey by your side.

To my precious children, Jordan and Mishan,

You are Mama's greatest "why". I promise to keep pressing, pushing and fighting each day to be a better version of me for you.

If I could write a letter to my younger self, it will read two candid and compelling lines:

"Dear Maggie,

Thank you for pressing on.

Thank you for rising through the ashes to be the woman you are today."

Now, to you, dear reader, I leave these five keys, five non-negotiables, or five don'ts:

1. Do not settle.
2. Do not underestimate.
3. Do not overshare.
4. Do not forget.
5. Do not ever give up.

Do not settle: Settling means embracing the four walls and the comfort of the status quo as all you can have, be, or aspire to. There is so much more to be attained than what we have been conditioned to as the norm. Never settle for another person's vision of who you are, what you can do, and how far you can go in life. Do not settle for safe. On the stage of life, at home, work, or play, show up. Participate. Engage. You are so much more than anything, good or bad, that has ever happened to you. **DARE.**

Do not underestimate yourself or another based on race, age, nationality, or gender. You'd be surprised just how quickly things can change in someone's favor to the detriment of another.

Do not overshare: As the saying goes, "some things are better left unsaid." Do not unveil all of your plans, hopes, and aspirations too early. There is a Turkish proverb that says:

> *"The forest was shrinking but the trees kept voting for the axe as its handle was made of wood and they thought it was one of them."*

You never know who in the crowd could hijack and run faster with your nascent idea than you would have time to fundraise.

Discretion is essential on the journey of life.

Do not forget: Everything happens in life for a reason; the good, the bad, and the ugly. Do not forget the lessons life is teaching you through each of these experiences. Also, do not forget who helped you along the way. No one makes it on their own. Your journey will be filled with people who will walk into your life for a reason, a season, or the entire journey towards destiny. Do not forget them. Your paths may diverge along the road for various reasons, but rest assured, they would have played a part in pushing you along on the swing of life. Do not forget them.

Do not give up: No matter how long it takes, how hard you have to try, don't you ever give up. Never be afraid to unlearn, excavate, dig up, and rediscover "who you were before the world got its hands on you[123]." Always remember,

> *"Anything that annoys you is teaching you patience. Anyone who abandons you is teaching you how to stand up on your own two feet. Anything that angers you is teaching you forgiveness and compassion. Anything that has power over you is teaching you how to take your power back. Anything you hate is teaching you unconditional love. Anything you fear is teaching you courage to overcome your fear. Anything*

you can't control is teaching you how to let go and trust the Universe[124]."

For however long you cry, and for however many times you fail, make sure to dust off and get back up again. Life is a ferry; never be so focused on the destination that you forget to enjoy the ride. Look around you, take in the scenes; miracles are happening around you each day. Take notice. No matter what comes, know that you will be okay. You will work through the mess, and in the end, a beautiful message will emerge.

Lastly, to all the "She's" of this world, indomitable lionesses, this is my wish for you:

"I hope you live louder.

I hope you laugh more.

I hope you sing at the top of your lungs.

I hope you drive with the windows down and let the wind rustle through your hair.

I hope you hug.

I hope you kiss.

I hope you surround yourself with people who make you feel alive.

I hope you become the type of person that brings good energy wherever you go,

and the type of person people want to be around.

I hope you speak what's on your mind, that you raise your voice for injustice, and that you tell others that you love them, instead of waiting until it's too late.

I hope you live louder, shine brighter.
From this moment on[125]."

Now go out there and LIVE!

With heartfelt admiration,

Maggie

Conclusion

What If We Healed as a Nation?

"I raise up my voice- not so I can shout, but so that those without a voice can be heard[126]."

Malala Yousafzai, Nobel Laureate

As I conclude my thoughts on this elaborate introspective catharsis, I can't help but realize that there seems to be an interesting parallel between my life story and that of Mama Liberia.

1. We are both women struggling to heal from scars of abuse at the hands of people we trusted.

2. We are both women whose trajectory started very differently from the path we now find ourselves on.

3. We are both strong African women seeking to find our place in the world while creating firm footing for our children to stand on.

As intensely passionate women, like tropical mangoes, we are fragile to the touch but resilient to the core. It doesn't take much to love us, and when we love, we love sincerely and unreservedly. I am humbled by the realization that my country and I have more in common than I could have ever imagined. As kindred spirits, how do we both find the courage to heal from the harm done to our souls? How do we celebrate the inherent beauty in our broken pieces? How can we sit on our proverbial mat and wrap our hands around each other in the comforting embrace of empathy? How do we attain a place of higher consciousness? How do we practicalize kintsugi? Nelson Mandela once said:

> *"When a deep injury is done to us, we never heal until we forgive[127]."*

Since the aim of this process is attaining closure, let me go first. I, Magdalene A. Matthews Ofori-Kuma, daughter of Baccus and Helena, release my heart of every hurt, hate, ache, and concealed shrapnel buried in my soul from the theft of my innocence. I accept the apology I never received. I willingly, consciously, and publicly set myself free from any hold, physical, emotional, spiritual, and psychological, that horrendous experience may have had over my life. As hard, as painful, and as near impossible as this uphill climb to wholeness has been, I forgive.

I forgive.

I forgive.

I forgive.

I forgive.

Now, it is your turn, Mama Liberia. For all the needs Liberia has, the nation's greatest need moving into the future is true national reconciliation. Generations since her founding, nearly two decades since the end of the civil conflict, and genuine reconciliation is yet to take root in the national psyche. The echoes of Liberia's historical legacy continue to resonate. The nation and her children remain trapped in a vicious cycle of "us vs. them" as hearts continue to bleed.

What if we healed as a nation?

What if we invested resources and political will and paid serious attention to national reconciliation? The delayed, untenable attempt to reunite the nation was a massive missed opportunity in the last two decades. Yet, all is not lost. What if we decided, despite competing demands, that true national reconciliation would be the one thing we prioritize in this new decade? Again, it was Madiba that said:

> "In the end, reconciliation is a spiritual process, which requires more than just a legal framework. It has to happen in the hearts and minds of people[128]."

The Truth and Reconciliation Commission made us revisit the past and get to the truth through various testimonies and experiences. It fell short on the reconciliation part of things, achieving accountability and mending the brokenness in the soul of the nation and her people. Due to our collective failure to implement the recommendations emerging from the extensive 5-year TRC process, we failed to build upon the momentum from post-conflict to recovery and ensure that the new Liberia was reborn on a clean slate. That ship has sailed—yes. But what if we took all that was uncovered, all that was uncovered during that extensive exercise, and tried to move through to a place of healing?

What if we healed as a nation?

I take a step further and analyze the current global racial reckoning in the United States against Liberia's own messy ethnic, Congo-Country, dichotomy. There too, I see the two nations have more in common than meets the eye. They were both experiments in self-determination that ended up not being as inclusive as they should have been from the start.

There are multiple lessons to be teased out of the Liberian experience. On issues of race in America, as with ethnicity in Liberia, there is a cry for equality. Whether it is during the NFL games, in Fortune 500 companies, in North-South trade deals, in local communities, across the grappling health facilities, or at the ballot box, there is a cry for healing in both nations.

What if America considered dialogue, or what Liberians call a *"palava hut[ac]"* approach? A pseudo-Truth and Reconciliation Commission, developed on human-centered design, seeking to harmonize and craft a way forward for the many historical wrongs done to the black, brown, and Native-American communities in the United States. A national catharsis, which, if nothing else, provides a platform where people are "able to talk about it," space for people to be heard, listened to, acknowledged, and shown empathy. A community-led dialogue that provides an emotional outlet for centuries of pent-up pain. Legislating a federally-mandated, grassroots-managed TRC across the US, retracing the 400-year journey of black Americans, and revisiting the painful events leading up to and after the civil rights movement in the United States may be one step forward towards national healing. Another approach would

---

ac "The "Palava Hut" is a traditional alternative justice and accountability approach that is indigenous to the linguistic and ethnic strata of Liberia. As its name depicts, the Palava Hut was originally a specific structure or place where people of a community gathered to discuss matters that concerned their general welfare, whether they were matters related to justice, territorial and human security, land and misdemeanor, among others. With the unfolding of time, the Palava Hut gradually evolved from its original physical structural status to a conceptual arena that is evocable wherever and whenever desired, thus making it an integral trait of the cultural and traditional mentalities of the linguistic and ethnic communities of the country. The Palava Hut can at best be described as a system of very serious discussions and decisions in the common interest of a community or a group of persons, rather than just a physical edifice as was the case." Source: The Independent National Commission on Human Rights, https://inchrliberia.com/index.php/incidents/projects/brief-history

be to revisit the school curricula across the various states and develop a harmonized narrative of American history that considers the shared experiences of all Americans, regardless of how controversial and politically unsettling that account might be. As Maya Angelou surmised:

"Won't it be wonderful when black history and native American history and Jewish history and all of US history is taught from one book? Just US history[129]."

The American public-school curriculum provides electives for Native Indian, White American, Chicano, and Black History. As inclusive as this seems, this creates the opportunity for students to choose the version of history most palatable to one's race. Recent events, however, show that this selective narrative of history results in ill-informed, jaded generations, oblivious to the historical injustices and unsympathetic to the current lived experiences of others. Author of *The Blood of Emmett Till,* Timothy B. Tyson, writes:

"If there is to be reconciliation, first there must be truth[130]."

True historical accounts must be shared, as uncomfortable as they may be, for there to be true reconciliation and healing.

If there is anything to be learned from the continued divided Liberian experience, it is that a TRC or nation-wide dialogue on its own, for the sake of it, is not enough. The TRC is only useful if it yields concrete, meaningful recommendations and accountability measures that are, in turn, implemented. Healing and reconciliation must be backed by accountability and sustainable platforms for equity. Action must follow.

In the words of Archbishop Desmond Tutu of South Africa, another nation that turned to the TRC structure to facilitate healing at the end of apartheid,

> *"True reconciliation is never cheap, for it is based on forgiveness which is costly. Forgiveness in turn depends on repentance, which has to be based on an acknowledgment of what was done wrong, and therefore on disclosure of the truth. You cannot forgive what you do not know*[131]*."*

The process itself was a significant milestone in Liberia's recent history and an initial step towards recovery. Its weakness rested in the nation's failure to act. All the experiences shared, all the lessons learned, all the wounds reopened, all the lives lost, all the pain relived during the extensive testimonial and fact-finding process must be allowed to find closure in the gentle arms of decisive action.

Action that says you were heard, you were acknowledged, your experience, your hurt, your heart matter. As a nation, we have decided to validate your pain, address the biases crafted within our legal, public health, economic, political, and justice systems, and create a more equitable democracy that caters to the needs of the many as well as the few.

What if we really did strive to heal as nations?

In Memoriam

In loving memory of my dear friend

Sylvia Esinam Akonai-Otoo

January 23, 1985 – January 27, 2021

Thank you for 15 years of an incredible friendship.

Rest in power.

Cited Works

1 Sarah Noffke Quote, Pinterest, https://www.pinterest.
co.uk/pin/383791199493674996/ accessed February 2021
2 Independence Speech, Kwame Nkrumah, The Ghana
Reader: History, Culture, Politics, Edited by Kwasi Konadu;
Clifford C. Campbell, Duke University Press, DOI: https://
doi.org/10.1215/9780822374961
3 Ellen Johnson Sirleaf, This Child Will Be Great, Harper-
Collins, USA
4 Brian Shellum, (2018), African American Officers in Liberia: A Pestiferous Rotation, 1910–1942, Potomac Books
5 The African American Mosaic, Library of Congress:
https://www.loc.gov/exhibits/african/afam002.html#:~:-
text=The%20American%20Colonization%20Society%20
(ACS,the%20independent%20nation%20of%20Liberia.
accessed February 2021
6 The American Colonization Society, http://personal.deni-
son.edu/~waite/liberia/history/acs.htm accessed February
2018
7 American Colonization Society, Britannica: https://www.
britannica.com/topic/American-Colonization-Society accessed February 2021
8 The Portable Abraham Lincoln, Penguin Books, 2009 –
page 51 History - 369 pages
9 American Colonization Society (1816-1964), BackPast:
https://www.blackpast.org/african-american-history/amer-
ican-colonization-society-1816-1964/ accessed February
2021
10 Ibid.
11 Ellen Johnson Sirleaf, This Child Will Be Great, HarperCol-
lins, USA
12 Ibid.
13 Liberia Bulletin, Issue No. 24, The 87th Annual Report of
the American Colonization Society, Feb. 1904,

https://books.google.com/books?id=v2VJAQAAMAAJ&p-g=RA6-PA4&lpg=RA6-PA4&dq=president+arthur+bar-clay+inaugural+address+liberia&source=bl&ots=jIE-jFCgAuQ&sig=ACfU3U1iX0NvmkFnCkL7AcpRS4Ri-Jr7FZQ&hl=en&sa=X&ved=2ahUKEwihsYb_r_TpAhVJuZ-4KHd8AAiUQ6AEwB3oECAgQAQ#v=onepage&q=presi-dent%20arthur%20barclay%20inaugural%20address%20liberia&f=false

14 Truth and Reconciliation Commission Preliminary Find-ings and Determinations: http://www.trcofliberia.org/re-sources/reports/final/volume-one_layout-1.pdf

15 On the Back of History, Lekpele M. Nyamalon, Poet and Author, published with permission from the author

16 Helene Cooper, The House on Sugar Beach

17 Ibid.

18 Samuel P. Jackson (2019), Rich Land, Poor Country, The Paradox of Poverty in Liberia, USA

19 Lekpele M. Nyamalon (2017), Scary Dreams, An Antholo-gy of the Liberian Civil War, Forte Publishing

20 'The Fight Against Corruption Is Not in Words': Full Text Of Liberia's Independence Day Orator, Gbowee's Speech, Front Page Africa: https://frontpageafricaonline.com/front-slider/the-fight-against-corruption-is-not-in-words-full-text-of-liberias-independence-day-orator-gbowees-speech/ accessed February 2021

21 Quotes, Goodreads: https://www.goodreads.com/work/quotes/2853438-the-gift accessed February 2021

22 "Senate Election results of Liberia, 1997". Interparlia-mentary Union for Democracy for everyone. 1997

23 The U.S. Refugee Resettlement Program, Migration Policy Institute: https://www.migrationpolicy.org/article/us-refugee-resettlement-program#6 accessed February 2021

24 The Holy Bible, New King James Version: 1 Corinthians 5:17-18, accessed February 2021

25 Reconciliation Sayings and Quotes, Wise Sayings; https://www.wiseoldsayings.com/reconciliation-quotes/ accessed February 2021

26 18 Inspiring Nelson Mandela Quotes, Mondetta Foundation, http://www.mondettacharityfoundation.org/18-inspiring-nelson-mandela-quotes/ accessed February 2021

27 Quotes by Ruskin Bond, Goodreads: https://www.goodreads.com/quotes/512037-and-when-all-the-wars-are-over-a-butterfly-will accessed February 2021

28 Quotable Quotes, Goodreads: https://www.goodreads.com/quotes/381646-nothing-is-more-powerful-than-an-idea-whose-time-has accessed February 2021

29 Chinese Proverbs, Goodreads, https://www.goodreads.com/quotes/2704080-the-best-time-to-plant-a-tree-was-20-years accessed February 2021

30 Liberia Peace Talks Open In Ghana-2003-06-04, VOA News:https://www.voanews.com/archive/liberia-peace-talks-open-ghana-2003-06-04 accessed February 2021

31 Arrest Warrant for Liberian Leader, BBC News: http://news.bbc.co.uk/2/hi/africa/2961390.stm accessed February 2021

32 Leymah Gbowee (2011), Mighty Be Our Powers, Beast Books, USA

33 Operation Shining Express, Wikipedia: https://en.wikipedia.org/wiki/Operation_Shining_Express#:~:text=Operation%20Shining%20Express%20was%20the,the%20Second%20Liberian%20Civil%20War. accessed February 2021

34 Foreigners Evacuated from Liberian Capital, CNN International: http://www.cnn.com/2003/WORLD/africa/06/09/liberia.evac/index.html accessed February 2021

35 Captain Hank Bracker, Salty & Saucy Maine, Goodreads: https://www.goodreads.com/quotes/tag/liberia accessed February 2021

36 Willam   Invictus FIND LINK

37 Clarence Budington Kelland Quotes, Goodreads: https://

www.goodreads.com/quotes/296045-my-father-didn-t-tell-me-how-to-live-he-lived accessed February 2021

38 A Psalm of Life by Henry Wadsworth Longfellow, Poetry Foundation: https://www.poetryfoundation.org/poems/44644/a-psalm-of-life accessed February 2021

39 Otto Von Bismarck Quotes, Goodreads: https://www.goodreads.com/quotes/424187-politics-is-the-art-of-the-possible-the-attainable accessed February 2021

40 People Get the Government They Deserve, Swift County Monitor-News: http://www.swiftcountymonitor.com/articles/2018/01/22/%E2%80%98people-get-government-they-deserve%E2%80%99 accessed February 2021

41 Ibid.

42 Ibid.

43 Edward G. Bulwer-lytton Quotes, Brainy Quote: https://www.brainyquote.com/quotes/edward_g_bulwerlytton_142668 accessed February 2021

44 Ellen Johson Sirleaf, Inaugural Address, January 16, 2006, http://www.pul.org.lr/doc/Inaugural%20Address%20of%20President%20Ellen%20Johnson%20Sirleaf_16%20January%202006.pdf

45 The 1847 Liberian Constitution http://crc.gov.lr/doc/CONSTITUTION%20OF%201847%20final.pdf

46 Rep. John Lewis: Voting Is 'The Most Powerful Non-Violent Tool We Have,' Politics, January 3, 2017,Huffpost: https://www.huffpost.com/entry/john-lewis-social-change-voting-rights_n_57f2bd99e4b0703f7590753e accessed February 2021

47 Nelson Mandela, Conversations with Myself, Nelson Mandela Foundation: https://www.nelsonmandela.org/content/page/conversations-with-myself-book-launch accessed February 2021

48 Gabriel Baccus Matthews, Ten Years After, Association of Liberian Journalists in the Americas: https://www.aljaonline.org/gabriel-baccus-matthews-ten-years-after/ accessed

February 2021

49 Ibid.

50 Chinua Achebe Quotes, Goodreads, https://www.go-odreads.com/quotes/1227714-until-the-lions-have-their-own-historians-the-history-of accessed February 2021

51 Speech Delivered by Gabriel Baccus Matthews, September 5, 2002, At The Ongoing National Peace and Reconciliation Conference at the Unity Conference Center (UCC),Virginia, Liberia, https://blojlu.wordpress.com/2009/08/28/speech-delivered-by-gabriel-baccus-matthews/

52 e.h poems, There's a History of Heartbreak, Mind Journal, https://themindsjournal.com/theres-a-history-of-heartbreak/ accessed February 2021

53 Nathaniel Hawthorne (1850) The Scarlet Letter, e-book, http://www.literatureproject.com/scarlet-letter/scarlet_1.htm accessed February 2021

54 Silence quotes, Goodreads: https://www.goodreads.com/quotes/tag/silence?page=2 accessed February 2021

55 Lorraine Nilon Quotes, Goodreads, https://www.go-odreads.com/author/quotes/17287756.Lorraine_Nilon#:~:-text=%E2%80%9CEmotional%20abuse%20is%20de-signed%20to%20undermine%20another's%20sense%20of%20self.&text=It%20stems%20from%20the%20abus-er's,understanding%20of%20their%20own%20signifi-cance.%20%E2%80%9D accessed February 2021

56 Leymah Gbowee, Warrior Princesses, June 29, 2020, Official Facebook Account: https://www.facebook.com/ley-mahgbowee/posts/4504417616238789 accessed February 2021

57 Ibid.

58 Sarah Jakes Roberts, Social Media Post, Official Facebook Account,https://web.facebook.com/SarahJakesRoberts/posts/1769596033187064:0?_rdc=1&_rdr accessed February 2021

59 The Balme Library: http://balme.ug.edu.gh/ accessed

February 2021

60 Maya Angelou Quotes, Goodreads: https://www.goodreads.com/quotes/93512-you-may-encounter-many-defeats-but-you-must-not-be accessed February 2021

61 Langston Hughes, Harlem, Poetry Foundation: https://www.poetryfoundation.org/poems/46548/harlem accessed February 2021

62 Joseph of Arimathaea, The Holy Bible: Luke 23:50-53, accessed February 2021

63 The Holy Bible, King James Version: Numbers 27, accessed February 2021

64 Chimamanda Adichie, Professor James Niwoye Adichie, Facebook post, https://www.facebook.com/watch/?v=712494952678306

65 Vinati Bhola Quotes, Goodreads, https://www.goodreads.com/quotes/9242417-i-was-not-born-with-roses-in-my-chest-to accessed February 2021

66 Hope Quotes, Goodreads: https://www.goodreads.com/quotes/tag/hope accessed February 2021

67 Jamie Anderson Quotes, Goodreads: https://www.goodreads.com/quotes/9657488-grief-i-ve-learned-is-really-just-love-it-s-all-the#:~:text=Quotes%20%3E%20Quotable%20Quote-,%E2%80%9CGrief%2C%20I've%20learned%2C%20is%20really%20just%20love,with%20no%20place%20to%20go.%E2%80%9D accessed February 2021

68 Jeremiah 12:5, King James Bible, accessed February 2021

69 Resilience Quotes, Goodreads: https://www.goodreads.com/quotes/tag/resilience?page=1 accessed February 2021

70 Situation report,WHO: https://www.who.int/docs/default-source/coronaviruse/situation-reports/20200621-covid-19-sitrep-153.pdf?sfvrsn=c896464d_2 accessed February 2021

71 John Paul II, Address to the U.N., October 2, 1979 and

October 5, 1995". Vatican.va. Retrieved 2012-07-07. https://www.vatican.va/roman_curia/secretariat_state/2003/documents/rc_seg-st_20031210_human-rights_en.html

72 Universal Declaration of Human Rights, United Nation:https://www.un.org/en/universal-declaration-human-rights/ accessed February 2021

73 Martin Luther King, Jr. Quotes, Goodreads: https://www.goodreads.com/quotes/107324-we-have-flown-the-air-like-birds-and-swum-the accessed February 2021

74 Washington Irving Quotes, Goodreads: https://www.goodreads.com/quotes/22416-there-is-in-every-true-woman-s-heart-a-spark-of accessed February 2021

75 Paulo Coelho Quotes, Goodreads: https://www.goodreads.com/quotes/32466-before-a-dream-is-realized-the-soul-of-the-world accessed February 2021

76 William Shakespeare, Sonnet 29, Poetry Foundation, https://www.poetryfoundation.org/poems/45090/sonnet-29-when-in-disgrace-with-fortune-and-mens-eyes accessed February 2021

77 Adversity quotes, Goodreads: https://www.goodreads.com/quotes/tag/adversity?page=2 accessed February 2021

78 Jennifer Elisabeth Quotes, Goodreads: https://www.goodreads.com/author/quotes/8346165.Jennifer_Elisabeth accessed February 2021

79 Melissa Brown, Picturing Perfect, Goodreads: https://www.goodreads.com/quotes/1260105-once-in-a-while-in-the-middle-of-an-ordinary accessed February 2021

80 Danielle Bernock Quotes, Goodreads: https://www.goodreads.com/quotes/7003849-trauma-is-personal-it-does-not-disappear-if-it-is#:~:text=It%20does%20not%20disappear%20if%20it%20is%20not%20validated.,the%20screams%20healing%20can%20begin.%E2%80%9D accessed February 2021

81 Maya Angelou, Goodreads: https://www.goodreads.com/author/quotes/3503.Maya_Angelou accessed February 2021

82 Jennifer Elizabeth Quotes, Goodreads: https://www.goodreads.com/quotes/1277854-i-met-a-boy-whose-eyes-showed-me-that-the accessed February 2021

83 Osho Quotes, Goodreads: https://www.goodreads.com/author/quotes/2856822.Osho accessed February 2021

84 Sarah Jakes Roberts, Social Media Post, April 22, 2020, Official Facebook Account accessed February 2021https://www.facebook.com/139818882831462/photos/a.148568831956467/2126337660846231/

85   Ibid.

86 ArchBishop Nicholas Duncan Williams

87 J.R.R. Tolkien Quotes, Goodreads: https://www.goodreads.com/quotes/229-all-that-is-gold-does-not-glitter-not-all-those accessed February 2021

88 James N. Watkins Quotes, Goodreads: https://www.goodreads.com/quotes/9603610-a-river-cuts-through-rock-not-because-of-its-power accessed February 2021

89 The Mandela Washington Fellowship, Young African Leaders Initiative: https://yali.state.gov/mwf/ accessed February 2021

90 Barack Obama (2015). Administration of Barack Obama, 2015 Remarks at the Mandela Washington Fellowship for Young African Leaders, Presidential Summit Town Hall and a Question-and-Answer Session, August 3, 2015 https://www.google.com/url?sa=t&source=web&rct=j&url=https://www.gpo.gov/fdsys/pkg/DCPD-201500545/pdf/DCPD-201500545.pdf&ved=2ahUKEwi61tj_gLDvAh-VpTxUIHbGwDsAQFjAIegQIChAC&usg=AOvVaw0DUAF2m-cqdI9p-J27yofT2 accessed February

91 'I Don't Believe In Limits.' Marathoner Eliud Kipchoge On Breaking the 2-Hour Barrier by Sean Gregory, Time Magazine, October 22, 2019, TIME: https://time.com/5707230/eliud-kipchoge/ accessed February 2021

92 Winston Churchill Quotes, Goodreads: https://www.goodreads.com/quotes/537399-success-is-the-ability-to-go-from-

failure-to-failure accessed February 2021

93 Tyler Perry, I Don't Believe We Ever Fail, November 17, 2014, Social Media Post, Official Facebook Account, https://www.facebook.com/permalink.php?story_fbid=10153050579488268&id=121492378267 accessed February 2021

94 Lysa TerKeurst Quotes, QuoteFancy: https://quotefancy.com/quote/855865/Lysa-TerKeurst-Scars-are-beautiful-when-we-see-them-as-glorious-reminders-that-we accessed February 2021

95 Kathleen Tessaro, Rare Objects, Goodreads: https://www.goodreads.com/quotes/search?q=kintsugi#:~:-text=%E2%80%9Cthe%20point%20of%20kintsugi%20is,shouldn't%20be%20considered%20ugly. accessed February 2021

96 Jo Ann V. Glim, Begotten With Love: Every Family Has Its Story, Goodreads: https://www.goodreads.com/quotes/search?q=kintsugi#:~:text=%E2%80%9Cthe%20point%20of%20kintsugi%20is,shouldn't%20be%20considered%20ugly. accessed February 2021

97 Kintsugi quotes, Goodreads: https://www.goodreads.com/quotes/8717008-the-point-of-kintsugi-is-to-treat-broken-pieces-an accessed February 2021

98 16 Days of Activism Against Gender-based Violence, UN Women:https://www.unwomen.org/en/news/in-focus/end-violence-against-women/2018 accessed February 2021

99 Elizabeth Ohene, Why I went public about being raped, 67 years later, October 12, 2019, BBC News: https://www.bbc.com/news/world-africa-50014745 accessed February 2021

100 Warrior Princesses, Leymah Gbowee, Official Facebook Page: https://www.facebook.com/leymahgbowee/posts/4504417616238789 accessed February 2021

101 Iyanla Vanzant Quotes, Goodreads: https://www.goodreads.com/quotes/1015925-until-you-heal-the-wounds-of-your-past-you-are accessed February 2021

102 Recovering from Rape and Sexual Trauma, Melinda Smith, M.A. and Jeanne Segal, Ph.D. Last updated: October 2019, Helpguide: https://www.helpguide.org/articles/ptsd-trauma/recovering-from-rape-and-sexual-trauma.htm accessed February 2021

103 15 Ways to Heal After Experiencing Sexual Assault, According to Professionals, Hayley Macmillen, NOV 10, 2016, Cosmopolitan: https://www.cosmopolitan.com/sex-love/a8272789/healing-after-sexual-assault/ accessed February 2021

104 T.D. Jakes Quotes, QuoteFancy https://quotefancy.com/quote/945655/T-D-Jakes-I-found-out-that-the-things-that-hurt-us-the-most-can-become-the-fuel-and-the accessed February 2021

105 Kintsugi Quotes, Candice Kumai, Goodreads: https://www.goodreads.com/quotes/search?q=kintsugi accessed February 2021

106 Shannon L. Adler Quotes, Goodreads: https://www.goodreads.com/quotes/1261463-forget-what-hurt-you-in-the-past-but-never-forget#:~:text=%E2%80%9CForget%20what%20hurt%20you%20in%20the%20past%2C%20but%20never%20forget,didn't%20learn%20a%20thing. accessed February 2021

107 Steve Maraboli Quotes, Goodreads: https://www.goodreads.com/quotes/318941-the-truth-is-unless-you-let-go-unless-you-forgive accessed February 2021

108 The Caged Bird by Maya Angelou, Goodreads: https://www.goodreads.com/search?utf8=%E2%9C%93&q=opens+his+throat+to+sing&search_type=quotes accessed February 2021

109 Leymah Gbowee Quotes, Goodreads: https://www.goodreads.com/quotes/8664426-you-can-never-leave-footprints-that-last-if-you-are accessed February 2021

110 Roy T. Bennet Quotes, Goodreads: https://www.goodreads.com/quotes/8014046-the-biggest-wall-you-

have-to-climb-is-the-one#:~:text=Quotes%20%3E%20
Quotable%20Quote-,%E2%80%9CThe%20biggest%20
wall%20you%20have%20to%20climb%20is%20the%20
one,%2C%20the%20rest%20will%20follow.%E2%80%9D
accessed February 2021

111 William Shakespeare Quotes, Goodreads: https://www.
goodreads.com/quotes/2056-cowards-die-many-times-be-
fore-their-deaths-the-valiant-never accessed February 2021

112 Vironika Tugaleva Quotes, Goodreads: https://www.go-
odreads.com/quotes/6138388-you-are-not-who-you-think-
you-are-you-are accessed February 2021

113   Toni Morrison Quotes, Goodreads: https://www.
goodreads.com/quotes/18179-freeing-yourself-was-one-thing-
claiming-ownership-of-that-freed#:~:text=%E2%80%9C-
Freeing%20yourself%20was%20one%20thing%2C%20claim-
ing%20ownership%20of%20that%20freed,%E2%80%95%20
Toni%20Morrison%2C%20Beloved accessed February 2021

114 Lord's Castle of Love and Hate, Standard, August 30,
2012, The Standard:https://www.standardmedia.co.ke/
business/article/2000065063/lord-s-castle-of-love-and-
hate accessed February 2021

115 The Holy Bible, New King James: Psalm 107:23-24, accessed February 2021

116 Anne Lammott Quotes, Mind Journal: https://the-
mindsjournal.com/wake-day-youre-65-75/ accessed February 2021

117 Bishop Jaqueline McCullough, Official Facebook
post:https://www.facebook.com/drjackiemccullough/
posts/10158454831705944 accessed February 2021

118 Paul Bloom Quotes, Brainy Quote: https://www.brainy-
quote.com/quotes/paul_bloom_644648
accessed February 2021

119 She Quotes, Goodreads: https://www.goodreads.com/
quotes/tag/she-quotes accessed February 2021

120 134 Inspiring Friendship Quotes, The positivity Blog:

https://www.positivityblog.com/friendship-quotes/ accessed February 2021
121 Fortitude Definition, Merriam-Webster Dictionary,
https://www.merriam-webster.com/dictionary/forti-
tude#:~:text=formal%20%3A%20mental%20strength%20
and%20courage,face%20danger%2C%20pain%2C%20etc.
accessed February 2021
122 Mel Robbins, Goodreads: https://www.goodreads.com/
quotes/8754088-you-have-been-assigned-this-mountain-
so-that-you-can accessed February 2021
123 Emily McDowell Quotes, Goodreads: https://www.
goodreads.com/quotes/9586181-finding-yourself-is-not-re-
ally-how-it-works-you-aren-t accessed February 2021
124 Jackson Kiddard Quote, Pinterest: https://www.pinter-
est.com/pin/168885054754272672/ accessed February 2021
125 The Quote Archive, Tiny Buddha Wisdom Quotes:
https://tinybuddha.com/wisdom-quotes/i-hope-you-live-
louder/ accessed February 2021
126 Malala Youfsafzai Quotes, Goodreads: https://www.good-
reads.com/quotes/850987-i-raise-up-my-voice-not-so-i-can-
shout-but accessed February 2021
127 18 Inspiring Nelson Mandela Quotes, Mondetta Charity Foundation, http://www.mondettacharityfoundation.
org/18-inspiring-nelson-mandela-quotes/ accessed February 2021
128 Nelson Mandela Quote, Quote Fancy, https://quotefan-
cy.com/quote/874477/Nelson-Mandela-In-the-end-recon-
ciliation-is-a-spiritual-process-which-requires-more-than
accessed February 2021
129 Maya Angelou Quotes, Brainy Quote, https://www.
brainyquote.com/quotes/maya_angelou_578792#:~:text=-
Maya%20Angelou%20Quotes&text=Won't%20it%20be%20
wonderful%20when%20black%20history%20and%20na-
tive,Just%20U.S.%20history. accessed February 2021
130 Quotes by Timothy B. Tyson, Goodreads: https://www.

goodreads.com/quotes/277663-if-there-is-to-be-reconcilia-tion-first-there-must-be accessed February 2021
131 Desmund Tutu Quotes, AZQuotes, https://www.azquotes.com/quote/1446609 accessed February 2021